0201510

D0615673

# CLIFFS NOTES

## Melville's

ON LINE

# Moby Dick

FICTION
Melvi
Melville, Herman

Moby Dick/Cliff Notes

aries

otes

*About the Author*

Stanley Baldwin is a writer and teacher living in Nebraska.

*Publisher's Acknowledgments*

*Editorial*

Project Editor: Tracy Barr

Acquisitions Editor: Greg Tubach

Glossary Editors: The editors and staff at Webster's New World Dictionaries

Editorial Administrator: Michelle Hacker

*Production*

Indexer: York Production Services, Inc.

Proofreader: York Production Services, Inc.

IDG Books Indianapolis Production Department

# Table of Contents

# How to Use This Book

CliffsNotes Melville's *Moby-Dick* supplements the original work, giving you background information about the author, an introduction to the novel, a graphical character map, critical commentaries, expanded glossaries, and a comprehensive index. CliffsNotes Review tests your comprehension of the original text and reinforces learning with questions and answers, practice projects, and more. For further information on Herman Melville and *Moby-Dick*, check out the CliffsNotes Resource Center.

CliffsNotes provides the following icons to highlight essential elements of particular interest:

Reveals the underlying themes in the work.

Helps you to more easily relate to or discover the depth of a character.

Uncovers elements such as setting, atmosphere, mystery, passion, violence, irony, symbolism, tragedy, foreshadowing, and satire.

Enables you to appreciate the nuances of words and phrases.

## Don't Miss Our Web Site

Discover classic literature as well as modern-day treasures by visiting the CliffsNotes Web site at www.cliffsnotes.com. You can obtain a quick download of a CliffsNotes title, purchase a title in print form, browse our catalog, or view online samples.

You'll also find interactive tools that are fun and informative, links to interesting Web sites, tips, articles, and additional resources to help you, not only for literature, but for test prep, finance, careers, computers, and Internet too. See you at www.cliffsnotes.com!

# LIFE AND BACKGROUND OF THE AUTHOR

## Early Years and Education

Herman Melville was born on August 1, 1819, the third of eight children. His father, Allan Melvill (the family changed the spelling of the last name around 1838) was of unsteady temperament but a prosperous importer and merchant in New York City. His mother, Maria Gansevoort, was a devoutly religious, somewhat critical woman from a colonial family of social standing in Albany. When Allan's fur and hat business began to fail, he moved it to Albany without success. The father died in 1832, bankrupt and apparently insane. The family moved to Lansingburgh in 1837 in an attempt to cut expenses.

Herman had a troubled childhood. A bout with scarlet fever at the age of seven left his eyesight permanently damaged, and, following his father's death, the family was so poor that Herman's education was sporadic. He studied the classics in Albany and trained to be a surveyor while in Lansingburgh but had to curtail his education to earn money for the family. Despite his weak eyes, Melville was an avid reader and delighted in finding, in his late twenties, an edition of Shakespeare with print large enough to accommodate him. But his real education was at sea. He could say, with Ishmael, "a whale-ship was my Yale College and my Harvard."

## Life at Sea and Marriage

Following brief stints as a clerk and schoolteacher, Melville signed on as a cabin boy with the trade ship *St. Lawrence* in 1839, completing a round trip to Liverpool. Upon his return, he again taught school, unsuccessfully sought work in New York City, and traveled on a Mississippi River steamboat. In January 1841, Melville's life took a significant turn as he sailed as a crew member on the American whaler *Acushnet*, taking the Cape Horn (southern tip of South America) route to the Pacific Ocean and the Marquesas Islands. There, in the summer of 1842, he and a friend jumped ship in response to the wretched conditions on board and the brutality of the ship's officers. Melville lived with friendly cannibals in the interior of Nuku Hiva for a month or so before joining the crew of the Australian whaler *Lucy Ann*. Melville's difficulty with the stern discipline aboard ships of the day continued. At Tahiti in September 1842, he and several other rebellious sailors refused to follow orders and were imprisoned on land. Easily escaping a few weeks later, Melville sailed on an American whaler, the *Charles and Henry*, ending up in Hawaii where, in April 1843, he was discharged and worked as a clerk and a pinsetter in a bowling alley. He signed on with the U. S. Navy frigate *United States*, again visiting Tahiti and the Marquesas as well as various Latin American ports before being discharged in Boston in October 1844.

Approaching the age of thirty, Melville sought stability in a marriage (1847) to Elizabeth "Lizzie" Knapp Shaw, daughter of the Chief Justice of the Massachusetts Supreme Court and a friend of his sister Helen. Relying on borrowed money from his wife's family, Melville purchased a farm (1850), which he called Arrowhead, in Massachusetts. Nearby lived Nathaniel Hawthorne, fifteen years Melville's senior, who published his most famous novel, *The Scarlet Letter*, that year; the two became friends.

# Writing and Reputation

Melville's writing career, much of which was inspired by his travels, began with the publication of *Typee* in 1846, followed relatively shortly after by *Omoo* (1847). The reaction to these first two novels was encouraging enough to make Melville believe, initially, that he had a future as a professional writer. For a short time, contemporaries thought of him as one of the bright young novelists of America. These first two books are based on the author's experiences in the South Seas—*Typee* on his life with the cannibals and *Omoo* on his experiences in Tahiti. They purport to be fairly factual adventure stories allowing the audience an unusual view of Polynesian life, and each was a modest critical success.

*Mardi* (1849) was not. It opens with apparent realism as the narrator deserts his whaling ship, but it develops into a fantasy that readers rejected. Even Melville called it a "chartless voyage." Melville returned to the approach of his first two books in *Redburn* (1849), a partly autobiographical story of the reminiscences of a "Son-of-a-Gentleman" in the merchant service. Much of *White Jacket* (1850) is a fictional account of Melville's experiences aboard the U. S. frigate *United States*. The narrator exposes the tyranny and injustice of life aboard a warship, from the point of view of an enlisted man. Melville claimed that he wrote these two novels strictly for money, and they did have limited success.

Melville produced his finest book, *Moby-Dick,* in 1851. Only a few critics recognized the genius of the work, and Melville had serious doubts about his future career. *Pierre* (1852) was too ambiguous and complex for Melville's audience. The story, somewhat autobiographical, deals with a young writer who seeks strict honesty but finds only disaster for himself and those around him. *Israel Potter* (1855), somewhat more successful, was first published as a magazine serial. It is a rewrite of a story about an American Revolutionary veteran who returns to America after fifty years of adventures abroad, having learned to be a survivor through the application of good sense. *The Piazza Tales* (1856) contains some of Melville's finest writing, shorter works such as "Bartleby, the Scrivener," a consideration of the values of Wall Street; the dark "Benito Cereno"; and a work that has grown in respect over the years, "The Encantadas," a philosophical look into the Galapagos Islands. *The Confidence-Man* (1857), an enigmatic consideration of identity and self-deception taking place on a Mississippi River steamboat, was the last work of fiction that Melville published in his lifetime. These last works, especially *The Piazza Tales*, found some small audience, but Melville was terribly discouraged and withdrew from his efforts to support himself and his family through writing.

Despite his disappointment, Melville did continue to write part-time. During the final days of the Civil War, he created some moving poetry that he eventually published in *Harper's New Monthly Magazine* and in a volume titled *Battle-Pieces* (1866). A prose "Supplement" calls for decency on the part of the victorious North during the reconstruction period, a position that Abraham Lincoln espoused but did not live to bring into effect. Again, contemporary reviews were tepid.

Melville published three more books in his declining years, all at his own or a sponsor's expense. *Clarel* (1876) is a long poem based on his pilgrimage to the Holy Land. While ambitious, it does not attract many readers even today. *John Marr and Other Sailors* (1888) is a collection of poems based on Melville's life as a seaman. *Timoleon and Other Ventures in Minor Verse* (1891) is a collection of poetry partly based on his travels. These last two were handsome little private editions of only twenty-five copies each.

Melville left a few unpublished poems and, most notably, the fine novella *Billy Budd, Foretopman*, which was finally published in 1924. Although Melville was thought to be one of the finer young writers in America at the end of the 1840s, by his death he was nearly forgotten. Only one obituary noted his passing on September 28, 1891.

# INTRODUCTION TO THE NOVEL

# Introduction

In his "Introduction" to the 1998 Oxford World's Classic edition of *Moby-Dick*, Tony Tanner suggests that the novel could only have been written in America and only in the mid-nineteenth century. The country then "seemed to stand at a new height, or new edge, of triumphant dominion and expansionary confidence in the western world." Tanner and others point out that, during Melville's life, the United States emerged from a colonial society to a world power with its own significant history and mythology. There were also tremendous advances in technology—the development of the railroad, telegraph, and telephone enabling easier travel and communication. Democracy was on the rise, and the country was ready to produce literary voices of its own.

At the time that the novel was published, the terrible destruction of the Civil War was not yet imagined. In fact, the Compromise of 1850, originated by Kentucky's Senator Henry Clay, effectively postponed the conflict eleven years by admitting one territory as a free state (California) while allowing slave owners to populate others (Utah and New Mexico). It was a prosperous, optimistic time in America, but some scholars argue that this very frame of mind kept many readers away from Melville's most interesting work because the novel was too dark or complicated for its time. In letters to his friend Nathaniel Hawthorne, Melville himself discusses his difficulty in finding an adequate audience.

Tanner's salient point, though, is that America in the mid-nineteenth century was an ideal place and time to "generate its own epic and myth—in effect find its own Homer." A strong argument can be made for *Moby-Dick*'s being the first great American epic in its length, its elevated style, and its treatment of the trials and achievements of democratic heroes or epic anti-heroes of national and cultural significance. Tanner treats this possibility in detail.

Perhaps more to the point, however, is the importance of time and place to the emergence of a great book about whaling. As Charles Olson points out (*Call Me Ishmael*, 1947; excerpted in *Modern Critical Interpretations of* Moby-Dick, edited by Harold Bloom), of 900 whaling vessels on the seas in 1846, 735 were American. Americans had been whaling since colonial days, but the industry peaked in the United States in the 1840s. Nantucket Island and New Bedford, Massachusetts, were the most important whaling ports in the world. Sperm oil alone was processed in excess of five million gallons per year.

Melville had served as a crewman on a whaler and knew the profession well. Among other accurate details, he discusses the length of a voyage (two to three years), life aboard ship, the number of open boats in a given chase, and the crews on those boats: usually one officer, one harpooner, and four oarsmen per boat. He is able to find comic relief in standard procedures such as the method of payment and the shore life of crewmen.

Just a few years later, kerosene became popular as a cheap fuel for lamps, and excessive hunting began to destroy the schools of whales. In Chapter 105 of the novel, Ishmael expresses certainty that the whale will never be eliminated to the degree that the American buffalo had been. It is, he thinks, too difficult to find whales in the world's vast oceans. In only a few years, he would be proven wrong. The whale has become even more endangered in subsequent years.

The historical setting of the novel was essential. It contributed to the creation of a great book about whaling and perhaps to the writing of the first American epic.

# A Brief Synopsis

"Call me Ishmael," the narrator begins, in one of the most recognizable opening lines in American literature. This observant young man from Manhattan has been to sea four times in the merchant service but yearns for a whaling adventure. On a cold, gloomy night in December, he arrives at the Spouter-Inn in New Bedford, Massachusetts, and agrees to share a bed with a stranger. Both men are alarmed when the bunkmate, a heavily tattooed Polynesian harpooner named Queequeg, returns late and discovers Ishmael beneath his covers. But the two soon become good friends and decide to sail together from the historical port of Nantucket.

In Nantucket, they sign on with the *Pequod*, Queequeg the more attractive employee due to his excellence with the harpoon. Ishmael, lacking any further ambition, will be a common sailor. The ship's captain, Ahab, is nowhere to be seen; nevertheless, they hear of him. He is a "grand, ungodly, god-like man" (Chapter 16), according to one of the owners, a man of few words but deep meaning, who has been in colleges as well as among the cannibals. A raggedy prophet of doom named Elijah catches the two friends on the dock and hints at trouble with Ahab. The mystery grows on Christmas morning when Ishmael spots dark figures in the mist, apparently boarding the *Pequod* shortly before it sets sail.

The ship's officers direct the early voyage. The chief mate, Starbuck, is a sincere Quaker and fine leader. Second mate is Stubb, a prankster but an able seaman. Third mate is Flask, dull but competent. When Ahab finally appears on his quarter-deck one morning, he is an imposing, frightening figure whose haunted visage sends shivers over the narrator. A white scar, reportedly from a thunderbolt, runs down his face and, they say, the length of his body. He has a grim, determined look. One leg is missing and replaced by a prosthesis fashioned from a sperm whale's jaw.

Ahab finally gathers the crewmen together and, in a rousing speech, solicits their support in a single purpose for this voyage: hunting down and killing the White Whale—Moby Dick, a very large sperm whale with a snow-white head. Only Starbuck resists the charismatic, monomaniacal captain; the first mate argues repeatedly that the ship's purpose should be to gather whale oil and return home safely. Eventually, even Starbuck acquiesces.

The mystery of the dark figures is explained during the voyage's first chase, long before meeting Moby Dick. Ahab has secretly brought along his own boat crew, led by an ancient Asian named Fedallah, an inscrutable figure with an odd influence over Ahab. Later, while guarding a captured whale one night, Fedallah tells Ahab of a prophecy of his (Ahab's death).

Queequeg becomes deathly ill and orders a canoe-shaped coffin from the ship's carpenter. Just as everyone has given up hope, the island aborigine decides to live and soon recovers. The coffin serves as his sea chest and later is caulked and pitched to become the ship's life buoy. Queequeg heroically rescues two drowning men in the novel; his coffin will save a third.

There are numerous "gams" in the novel, social meetings of two ships on the open sea. Crews normally visit each other during a gam, captains on one vessel and chief mates on the other. Newspapers and mail are exchanged. The men talk of whale sightings or other news. For Ahab, however, there is but one relevant question to ask of another ship: "Hast seen the White Whale?" Some have. The captain of the *Samuel Enderby* lost an arm to the leviathan. The *Rachel* has also seen Moby Dick. As a result, one of its open boats is missing; the captain's son is aboard. The captain of the *Rachel* begs Ahab to aid in the search, but the *Pequod*'s captain is resolute. He is very near the White Whale now and will not stop to help.

Ahab is the first to spot Moby Dick. For three days, the crew pursues the great whale, who repeatedly turns on the *Pequod*'s boats, wreaking destruction and killing Fedallah, sinking the *Pequod*, and dragging Ahab into the sea and his death. Only Ishmael survives, clinging to Queequeg's coffin. He floats for a day and a night before the *Rachel* rescues him.

# List of Characters

**Ishmael**  The narrator of the novel is a keen observer, a young man with an open mind who is wary of Ahab but, like most of the crew, swept away by the captain's charisma.

**Ahab**  The "grand, ungodly, god-like man" is a deeply complex figure, one of the most controversial in American literature. His monomaniacal hunt for Moby Dick dominates the novel's plot.

**Moby Dick**  The giant sperm whale seems to manipulate his confrontations with mankind in a manner beyond the capacity of a leviathan. Critics debate the nature of Moby Dick: whether he is an allegorical representation of some eternal power, a representation of Ahab's obsession, or nothing more, literally, than a whale.

**Queequeg**  The Polynesian harpooner who opens Ishmael's mind and eventually—and indirectly—saves his life. Queequeg is important to the theme of friendship and the value of diversity.

**Father Mapple**  His sermon at the Whaleman's Chapel sets the tone for the novel. The message, through the story of Jonah, is that we must disobey our own desires if we are to learn to obey God.

**Starbuck**  The chief mate aboard the *Pequod*. He is the only one who attempts to stand up to Ahab's obsessive direction of the ship's purpose. Even he eventually acquiesces.

**Fedallah** The ancient Asian who is Ahab's harpooner and spiritual guide. His prophecy regarding Ahab's death ominously foreshadows the end of the novel.

**Pip** The cabin boy, who nearly drowns when he is abandoned during a whale hunt. He discovers painful insights that allow him an unusual view of reality and temporarily endear him to Ahab.

**Elijah** The cryptic prophet who helps to set an early tone of dark mystery in the novel. He alerts Ishmael to possible problems with Ahab and secrets aboard the *Pequod*.

**Stubb** The second mate. He considers himself to be quite the wit, but his treatment of Fleece, the cook, is more cruel and racist than it is amusing.

**Perth** The ship's blacksmith. His story is an unusual departure for Melville as it is told with the excessive sentimentality and predictability of melodrama.

**Gabriel** The raving Shaker prophet aboard the *Jeroboam*. He correctly predicts Ahab's final resting-place.

**Bildad** A hypocritical Quaker. The co-owner's exchange regarding Ishmael's pay allows Melville an opportunity for a little caustic satire.

# Character Map

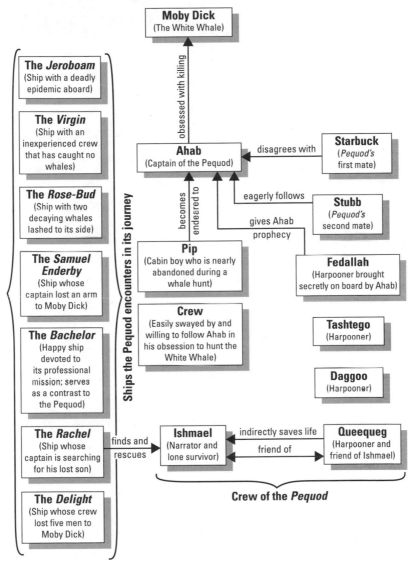

**Moby Dick**
(The White Whale)

**The *Jeroboam***
(Ship with a deadly epidemic aboard)

**The *Virgin***
(Ship with an inexperienced crew that has caught no whales)

**The *Rose-Bud***
(Ship with two decaying whales lashed to its side)

**The *Samuel Enderby***
(Ship whose captain lost an arm to Moby Dick)

**The *Bachelor***
(Happy ship devoted to its professional mission; serves as a contrast to the Pequod)

**The *Rachel***
(Ship whose captain is searching for his lost son)

**The *Delight***
(Ship whose crew lost five men to Moby Dick)

Ships the Pequod encounters in its journey

obsessed with killing

**Ahab**
(Captain of the Pequod)

disagrees with

**Starbuck**
(*Pequod's* first mate)

eagerly follows

**Stubb**
(*Pequod's* second mate)

gives Ahab prophecy

becomes endeared to

**Pip**
(Cabin boy who is nearly abandoned during a whale hunt)

**Fedallah**
(Harpooner brought secretly on board by Ahab)

**Crew**
(Easily swayed by and willing to follow Ahab in his obsession to hunt the White Whale)

**Tashtego**
(Harpooner)

**Daggoo**
(Harpooner)

finds and rescues

**Ishmael**
(Narrator and lone survivor)

indirectly saves life

friend of

**Queequeg**
(Harpooner and friend of Ishmael)

**Crew of the *Pequod***

# CRITICAL COMMENTARIES

# Chapters 1–2

# Loomings; The Carpet-bag

## Summary

As the novel opens, the narrator, a young man called Ishmael, expresses a yearning to lift his spirits with a sea voyage. Carrying only a change or two of clothing, he leaves his home in Manhattan and arrives in New Bedford, Massachusetts, on a cold Saturday night in December. From there, he hopes to catch a small boat to the historical port of Nantucket in order to sign on with a whaling ship. Unfortunately, there is no passage to Nantucket until Monday so he must find lodging that he can afford. He finally settles on the Spouter-Inn, Peter Coffin proprietor.

## Commentary

**Character Insight**

The novel opens with one of the most famous first lines in American literature: "Call me Ishmael." The biblical Ishmael (Genesis 16:1–16; 21:10 ff.) is disinherited and dismissed from his home in favor of his half-brother Isaac. The name suggests that the narrator is something of an outcast, a drifter, a fellow of no particular family other than mankind (foreshadowing the very last word of the novel's epilogue). Ishmael confirms his independent ways when he tells us that he never travels the ocean as a passenger because passengers tend to rely on others, becoming seasick or having other problems; worse, they must buy their passage instead of being paid. Nor does he seek any special rank aboard ship, neither captain nor cook, because he abominates "all honorable, respectable toils" and has enough trouble just taking care of himself. Because this novel presents such a strong first-person narrative voice, the reader can expect that this will be Ishmael's story as well as Moby Dick's or Ahab's or anyone else's. We might also remember that the narrator is Ishmael, not Melville.

We soon learn that Ishmael is a narrator who is open to the complexities of life. Others may accept simple explanations; Ishmael does not. *Moby-Dick* deals with depths and complications of meaning, presented primarily through the narrator. Ishmael is, above all, an observer. He avoids responsibility for others but genuinely cares for his friends. He doesn't mind servile occupations. After all, he says, "Who ain't a slave? Tell me that."

**Style & Language**

There is an ominous atmosphere in the setting of New Bedford on this frosty, wind-swept December night. The streets are nearly deserted, dreary blocks of blackness, only a solitary light flickering here or there, "like a candle moving about in a tomb." Ishmael is alone. The name of the inn where he finds a kind of shelter is reminiscent of the whaling industry; the proprietor's name foreshadows death. Ishmael is justified in being a bit wary, even afraid.

## Glossary

(Here and in the following glossary sections, difficult words and phrases, as well as allusions and historical references, are explained.)

**hypos**  here, hypochondria, imaginary illnesses.

**Manhattoes**  residents of Manhattan Island, New York City.

**circumambulate**  to walk around.

**lee**  leeward, downwind, on the sheltered side.

**salt**  here, an experienced sailor.

**forecastle**  the front part of the ship where the crew's quarters are located.

**Leviathan**  a sea monster, a whale (biblical).

# Chapter 3

# The Spouter-Inn

## Summary

Upon entering the inn, Ishmael is fascinated by a large, obscure oil painting. Eventually he decides that the subject is a ship foundering in a hurricane as a leaping whale is about to impale itself on the craft's three mastheads. After supper, finding no private beds available, Ishmael chooses to sleep on a bench, but that proves to be much too uncomfortable. Upon the urging of Mr. Coffin, the proprietor, Ishmael agrees to share a bed with a harpooner who is out attempting to sell an embalmed human head that the man obtained in the South Seas. Concerned but very weary, Ishmael retires. As he is nodding off, he is startled by the return of Queequeg, the harpooner who seems to Ishmael to be a monstrous cannibal. Queequeg is also surprised to find someone in his bed. Fearing for his life, Ishmael desperately hollers for the landlord's help.

## Commentary

Literary Device

The ominous tone continues as Ishmael enters the inn, which is compared to a condemned old ship. The narrator is quite taken by an obscure painting, a "boggy, soggy, squitchy picture" with such a confusion of shades and shadows that, for some time, Ishmael can make no sense of it. Contributing to the theme of death and foreshadowing later events in the novel, the subject seems to be a foundering ship under attack from a whale. As Ishmael's adventure continues, he will discover obscurity in many subjects, including life itself.

For this night, however, Ishmael seeks few solutions other than a hot meal and a place to sleep. Filled with meat and dumplings and unable to accommodate himself to a private bench, he accepts the landlord's suggestion that Ishmael share a bed with a harpooner.

The introduction of the harpooner Queequeg provides a comic interlude in what has been a gloomy night. Ishmael, however, is not laughing. Nor is Queequeg. Startled to find an apparent interloper in his bed, the heavily tattooed harpooner threatens homicide in a dialect that may seem stereotyped today but originally was intended to evoke humor as it adds to Ishmael's terror: "Who-e debel you? . . . you no speak-e, dam-me, I kill-e." Certain that he is about to be done in by a cannibal, Ishmael shouts for help. Mr. Coffin, enjoying the little trick he has pulled and confident that Queequeg is harmless, rushes in to settle the matter. Ishmael soon concludes that the harpooner is a decent, clean fellow and decides it is better to sleep with a sober cannibal than with a drunken Christian. This is just the beginning of Ishmael's understanding that the pagan Queequeg is a better man than most.

# Glossary

**bulwarks** the part of a ship's side above the deck.

**Cape-Horner** a ship that travels around Cape Horn at the southern tip of South America.

**skrimshander** scrimshaw, intricate carving of whalebones.

**tar** here, a sailor.

**obstreperously** noisily, boisterously.

**spliced** here, joined in marriage.

## Chapters 4–7

# The Counterpane; Breakfast; The Street; The Chapel

## Summary

Ishmael awakens first on Sunday morning and has time to observe the various tattoos on Queequeg's huge arm and face. The narrator wonders what sort of pagan he has for a bunkmate. When the harpooner finally stirs, however, he is thoughtful and kind, dressing first and leaving the room so Ishmael can have some privacy. After breakfast, Ishmael walks about New Bedford, winding up at Whaleman's Chapel where he notices numerous memorial tablets honoring men who died at sea. Ishmael thinks about death and immortality. He is a little surprised to see Queequeg in the congregation.

## Commentary

Under Queequeg's influence, Ishmael is opening his mind to the nature of mankind and the values to be found, if we bother to look, in people from diverse backgrounds. Initially frightened by the strange harpooner, the narrator is beginning to think of him as a friend, a more civilized man than most despite Queequeg's penchant for shaving with his harpoon and spearing the rarest steak for himself at breakfast—acts others might find barbaric even for a whaler. ("Civilized" folk in New England ate their meat well done in Melville's time and usually waited for the platter to pass.) The port city offers Ishmael more opportunities to observe people from other cultures: sailors from around the world, country dwellers, even real cannibals. He is beginning to enjoy the diversity of this world.

**Character Insight**

Ishmael and Queequeg's developing relationship is important to the allegorical concepts in the work. Initially, for example, Ishmael and Queequeg are perceived—by themselves and others—to be complete opposites: one civilized; the other a barbarian. Even the fact that Queequeg is dark and painted and Ishmael is fair seems to highlight this "oppositeness." And, in truth, the two men are opposites—in every way but the soul: If we scratch away the superficial descriptors, we see that each men is, essentially, like the other. Both are tolerant, both are decent. Both are forever helpful, and both are gentle people in an essentially brutal environment. Ishmael and Queequeg are universal characters that portray the best in man, and, as is made apparent later, they possess characteristics that Ahab lacks. Most significantly, Ishmael and Queequeg feel a love and responsibility for each other, and this is never more apparent than when Queequeg "saves" Ishmael at the end of the tale. Ahab, we will come to learn, has no connection to any other person or thing beyond the White Whale. Furthermore, he is willing to sacrifice anything (the *Pequod*, the profits from the successful hunts, his duty to the ship owners and his crew) and anybody, including the lives of every man aboard his vessel, for revenge.

At the chapel, Ishmael's thoughts turn to death and the question of what is important about life—what, if anything, survives after death. Because this little church primarily serves whalers, it prominently displays a number of memorial tablets honoring men killed at sea. Ishmael considers his own mortality and wonders if he will meet the fate of these men. His spirits rise, however, when he concludes that his physical self is not the real Ishmael at all. It is a shadow; and his shadow, his spirit, is his true substance. He concludes that we humans are like oysters at the bottom of the sea, limited in our view of reality. We are confused about what is important. In that frame of mind, he awaits the sermon.

## Glossary

**counterpane**  an embroidered quilt, here compared to Queequeg's tattooed skin.

**labyrinth**  an intricate network of winding passages, a maze.

**ablutions**  washing of the body, often ritualistic.

**eschewed**  avoided, shunned.

**bumpkin**  an awkward or simple person from the country.

**spermaceti**  a white, waxlike substance taken from the oil in the head of a sperm whale, used to make candles, cosmetics, or ointments.

## Chapters 8–9

# The Pulpit; The Sermon

## Summary

Father Mapple, an elderly but vigorous man of God, ascends to the pulpit by climbing a rope ladder like one used to mount a ship from a boat at sea. He was a harpooner in his youth, and he alludes to the imagery of seamen frequently in his sermon, referring to the congregation, for example, as his "shipmates." The pulpit itself is shaped like the prow of a ship and features a painting of a vessel battling a storm near a rocky coast, an angel of hope watching over it. The text for the sermon is the Old Testament's Book of Jonah, the story of Jonah and the whale.

## Commentary

The setting is the *Whaleman's* Chapel, and everything about it reminds the visitor of life and death at sea. Father Mapple is like the captain of the ship, the congregation his crew. When he enters the pulpit, he pulls the rope ladder up after him, symbolically cutting himself off, for the time, from worldly matters. This act foreshadows the way in which the *Pequod*, when set at sea, becomes its own microcosm (a symbolic little world), peopled by a diverse crew, isolated, captained not by the spiritual Father Mapple but by the troubled, rebellious, angry Ahab.

The sermon centers on the Old Testament story of Jonah and the whale. Its theme is that we must serve God by transcending our own self-interests: "And if we obey God, we must disobey ourselves; and it is in this disobeying ourselves, wherein the hardness of obeying God consists," Mapple states. This theme continues throughout the novel; the sermon sets its tone. The reader should remember this sermon in relationship to Ahab, who sins in numerous ways throughout the book but never repents and whose greatest sin is that he abjures all obligation to everything but his own desire for revenge.

The reader might recall that Ishmael concedes, early on in the book, that he has no problem serving a higher authority; we will discover that Ahab does. Jonah tries to flee his responsibility to God, but he finds that there is no place where God does not reign. Cast overboard during a storm at sea, Jonah is swallowed by a whale. Jonah's salvation comes only when he transcends his own desires and submits to God's will. Readers might profit from reviewing the short Book of Jonah, only four brief chapters—or "yarns" as Father Mapple calls them. Serious students of the novel certainly should study Mapple's sermon, in which, according to Mapple, are two great messages: The first message is do not sin, but, if you do, repent properly, not "clamoring for pardon, but grateful for punishment." The second, and the more awful, message is preach truth in the face of falsehood.

This chapter cements the connection between the physical and metaphysical, the worldly and the religious, the actual and the metaphoric. Jonah's story parallels Ahab's in that it represents man's relationship with his universe and his god(s). Jonah's approach was more God centered; Ahab's is more man centered.

## Glossary

**larboard** the left-hand side of the ship as one faces forward; also called *port*.

**starboard** the right-hand side of the ship as one faces forward.

**flouts** mocks or scoffs at, shows contempt for.

**cupidity** avarice, greed.

# Chapters 10–12
# A Bosom Friend; Nightgown; Biographical

## Summary

When Ishmael returns to his room after chapel, he finds Queequeg already there, carving on the nose of his small black idol, Yojo. After some friendly conversation, they bond by sharing a pipe of Queequeg's tobacco. Ishmael even joins the pagan in a burnt offering to Yojo. The narrator justifies his behavior by an allusion to the Golden Rule, which urges us to do unto others as we would want them to do unto us (Matthew 7:12). Queequeg shares his personal history, and the two roommates resolve to be shipmates.

## Commentary

The development of Ishmael's character continues as he opens his mind to Queequeg's character and background. Although the harpooner is a heathen, by Christian definition, Ishmael increasingly notices the man's independent dignity, good heart, and generous spirit. Despite outward appearances, Ishmael concludes, "You cannot hide the soul."

**Character Insight**

The harpooner is a native of Kokovoko (called Rokovoko in some chapters and editions), an island in the South Pacific where his father was king and his uncle a high priest. Ishmael has sensed his friend's noble spirit, with or without the pedigree. In fact, almost immediately Ishmael recognizes Queequeg's noble character, noting that he "treated me with so much civility and consideration, while I was guilty of great rudeness." Queequeg is a synthesis of all racial and ethnic characteristics; that is, he is a symbol of all mankind. His signature is the symbol for infinity.

The two men seal their bond by sharing a smoke from the harpooner's tomahawk pipe as well as a brief religious service honoring Queequeg's idol. After all, Queequeg has just attended a Christian service, which Ishmael appreciates; it seems only right to Ishmael to reciprocate. Opening his mind to religion is an important step for Ishmael, one which Queequeg took by leaving his home to sail the world and learn of Christians. The narrator mentions that both men are discovering that evil exists among Christians at least as much as among pagans. While this knowledge is somewhat disillusioning, it also expands their outlook and leads to a kind of wisdom that narrower minds miss.

## Glossary

**magnanimous** noble in mind, generous in overlooking insult or injury.

**confabulation** talking together in an informal way, chatting.

**ignominy** loss of one's reputation; dishonor, infamy.

**for the nonce** for now, for the time being.

**sceptre** rod or staff held by rulers on ceremonial occasions.

**hap** chance occurrence or event, especially an unfortunate one.

## Chapters 13–15

# Wheelbarrow; Nantucket; Chowder

## Summary

On Monday morning, the two friends check out of the Spouter-Inn and tote their belongings in a wheelbarrow to the *Moss*, a small schooner that will take them to Nantucket where they hope to sign on with a whaler. Queequeg recalls two anecdotes revealing cultural differences. Aboard the schooner, some louts mock Queequeg; one of them is taught a lesson but then saved from drowning by the huge harpooner. Arriving in Nantucket after dark, the friends quarter at Mr. Coffin's cousin's inn, the Try Pots, Mr. & Mrs. Hosea Hussey proprietors, and are treated to excellent clam chowder as well as cod chowder.

## Commentary

Ishmael continues to learn about the amazing Queequeg. Certain cultural distinctions broaden the two men's insights. The wheelbarrow reminds the harpooner of his introduction to a similar device shortly after he left the islands. Loaned a wheelbarrow to help him move his belongings from a ship to a boarding house, Queequeg loaded it and then lifted and *carried* the barrow and his gear up the wharf, to the amusement of onlookers. He recalls another humorous event, on his island home, when a visiting white captain of a merchant ship mistook a sacred punch for a finger bowl and washed his hands in the liquid. Cultural blunders depend so much on one's point of view.

**Character Insight**

Queequeg's depth of character is demonstrated in an incident aboard the *Moss* when some ignorant country bumpkins mimic him behind his back, one especially rude fellow making the mistake of getting caught. Queequeg tosses the lout into the air but guides his landing, causing the fellow more anxiety than injury. Just as the captain is reprimanding the harpooner for this, the same bumpkin is knocked overboard by a free-swinging boom. Only Queequeg dives into the icy waters to save him. In this dramatic fashion, Melville further contrasts the products of so-called "civilized" and "barbaric" cultures, the advantage clearly going to the pagan. Queequeg is a great man in any setting.

# Glossary

**packet** a boat that travels a regular route, carrying passengers, freight and mail.

**boom** a spar (pole) extending from a mast to hold the bottom of a sail outstretched.

**quohog** an edible clam having a large, thick, hard shell.

**chowder** a thick soup consisting of milk, various vegetables, salt pork, and clams or fish.

**try pots** vats used to melt or render whale blubber to get the oil.

# Chapter 16

# The Ship

## Summary

On Tuesday morning, Queequeg has a surprise for Ishmael. The harpooner says that his little black idol, Yojo, has informed him that Ishmael is to choose the whaling ship on which they will sail. After considering several vessels, the narrator selects the *Pequod* and negotiates with two of its owners, Captain Peleg and Captain Bildad, regarding enlistment and pay. The owners settle with Ishmael but are more enthusiastic about hiring Queequeg because he is an accomplished harpooner. Ahab, the ship's captain for the voyage, is not available but is briefly described.

## Commentary

**Literary
Device**

Although *Moby-Dick* is sometimes thought of as a deep, dark, serious novel, there are moments of delightful humor and even satire. This chapter is an example. Ishmael justifiably feels inadequate to the task of selecting a ship because it is Queequeg who has the whaling experience, but he rather comically accepts Yojo's authority and heads for the docks. He chooses the smallish *Pequod* (named after an extinct Massachusetts Indian tribe) because it is quaint, noble, even melancholy, all of which are virtues to Ishmael.

Melville has fun with the negotiations regarding Ishmael's pay. There is no set salary for the journey; each man is signed on for a fraction of the ship's profits, called a "lay." Although this is the narrator's first venture on a whaling ship, he has been to sea four times in the merchant service and anticipates a share of 1/275—about enough, he figures, to pay for his clothing—plus food and lodging aboard the ship. Bildad, a hypocritical Quaker, figures a 1/777 lay is plenty, reminding Ishmael of the biblical passage (Matthew 6: 19–21) warning those who *lay* up treasures for themselves on earth. With Peleg's intervention, they settle on 1/300. The elaborate satire of the hypocrite, Bildad, is consistent with Melville's ambiguous view of Christianity, which he respects when it is practiced sincerely but criticizes when it is not. Bildad pretends to be very concerned about Ishmael's soul and wouldn't want him corrupted by filthy old money, but he doesn't mind laying up treasures for himself!

The mysterious aura surrounding Ahab is suggested by his absence and increases with a brief description. He is, according to Peleg, "a grand, ungodly, god-like man," a man of few words but deep meaning who has "been in colleges, as well as @'mong the cannibals." He lost a leg to an "accursed whale" on his most recent voyage. A reference to the biblical Ahab (1 Kings 16:33), who "did more to provoke the Lord God of Israel to anger than all the kings of Israel that were before him," foreshadows a serious spiritual or *cosmic* struggle for it was *that* Ahab who denounced Jehovah (God) for the false god, Baal. All this is developed as the novel progresses.

## Glossary

**XXXIX Articles** the Articles of Faith of the Church of England.

**venerable** worthy of respect or reverence by reason of age and dignity or character.

**transom** here, a horizontal beam in the stern (rear) of the ship used as a seat.

**anomalous** deviating from the regular arrangement or general rule, abnormal.

**heterogeneous** opposite, dissimilar, incongruous.

**incorrigible** that cannot be corrected or improved.

**celerity** swiftness, speed.

## Chapters 17–20
# The Ramadan; His Mark; The Prophet; All Astir

## Summary

That evening, Ishmael waits until after dark to return to the room because Queequeg is fasting (a form of Ramadan) until sunset. The door is bolted from within. The landlady and Ishmael are concerned, and Ishmael breaks open the lock. Queequeg is fine but in a religious trance, which continues until dawn. That day, Queequeg signs on with the *Pequod*. Shortly after leaving the ship, the two friends are approached by a raggedy prophet of doom named Elijah who speaks of serious problems with Ahab. Ishmael judges the prophet a "humbug" (impostor). The ship is stocked and prepared for a long voyage.

## Commentary

While Ishmael tries to understand others' religions, he has difficulty accepting the extremes of what he sees as fanaticism, especially when health is threatened. He is equally opposed to Ramadan and the Christian Lent. Fasting, he argues, starves both the body and the soul, each of which thrives on sound digestion. Hell, he concludes, "is an idea first born on an undigested apple-dumpling"! His speech is wasted on Queequeg, who may be putting Ishmael on as he claims that his only indigestion occurred when his father's warriors killed fifty of the enemy in an afternoon and the tribe had barbecued and devoured them by evening.

Theme

The religious theme continues as the owners of the *Pequod* insist that Queequeg, whom they call "Quohog" (a kind of clam), must be a Christian in order to sail on their boat. Ishmael argues that Queequeg is a member of "the great and everlasting First Congregation of this whole worshipping world," a reference to the genuine spirituality and humanity of his friend. The owners accept Ishmael's "sermon" good-naturedly but are more impressed when Queequeg demonstrates his marksmanship with the harpoon. They sign him to a ninetieth lay.

In this context, the warnings of the shabbily dressed prophet of doom, Elijah, might well be dismissed as just another distortion of hypocrisy or spiritual fervor. Ishmael tries to treat them that way. Yet there is something legitimately foreboding about the stranger, which goes beyond humbug. He seems to know a good deal about Captain Ahab, whom he calls "Old Thunder," and makes references to various mysteries in the captain's past, including a deadly fight with a Spaniard and the loss of the leg. Ishmael and Queequeg will soon hear more from Elijah.

## Glossary

**Ramadan** the ninth month of the Muslim year, a period of daily fasting from sunrise to sunset; here, a reference to Queequeg's abbreviated religious fast.

**apoplexy** a brain hemorrhage or stroke, causing convulsions, paralysis, etc.

**sagacious** wise.

**dyspeptic** suffering from indigestion.

**abashed** embarrassed, ill at ease.

**Elijah** a biblical prophet of doom (1 Kings 21:17–19).

**ineffable** that cannot or dare not be put into words because too overwhelming or sacred.

## Chapters 21–23

# Going Aboard; Merry Christmas; The Lee Shore

## Summary

The *Pequod* is scheduled to sail on Christmas Day. In the gray pre-dawn mist, Queequeg and Ishmael approach the ship and think they see some figures boarding ahead of them. Elijah suddenly appears close behind and asks whether they have seen anyone going aboard. Ishmael says he thinks he saw four or five men, and Elijah challenges him to find them on the ship. Ishmael cannot. Nor is Ahab to be seen, though Ishmael is told by a sailor that the captain entered the vessel during the night. Peleg and Bildad help set the ship to sail and reluctantly return to land.

## Commentary

**Style & Language**

The aura of mystery surrounding the *Pequod* is enhanced by Ahab's absence and the unidentifiable figures who seem to be boarding the ship before dawn. Elijah toys with Ishmael through his cryptic statements, first insisting on a conversation and then offering only hints of his meaning. Typical is his farewell: "I was going to warn ye against—but never mind, never mind . . .. Shan't see ye again very soon, I guess; unless it's before the Grand Jury," an apparent suggestion of possible murder or mutiny during the voyage. Like the biblical Elijah, a prophet of the truth, *Moby-Dick*'s Elijah also speaks the truth, but in such a cryptic way that Ishmael, and the reader, is left to wonder at his meaning. Ishmael's uncertainty increases the more he knows, or doesn't know, about the trip. As a sensitive observer, he is aware of the unusual circumstances but still determined to have his whaling adventure.

The mood is lightened by the appearance of Peleg and Bildad, two old salts who act as if they would love to stay with the ship but have other responsibilities, most likely profitable ones, on land. Starbuck, the first mate, is briefly introduced and seems a steadying influence as he competently takes charge of the voyage in Ahab's absence.

# Glossary

**scuttle** here, a small, covered opening or hatchway in the outer hull or deck of a ship.

**aft** near or toward the stern (rear) of a ship.

**mainyard** the lowest rod or spar on the mainmast, from which the mainsail is set.

**intrepid** bold, fearless.

**apotheosis** deification or glorification of a person or thing.

**Lee Shore** the leeward, downwind, sheltered, or protected shore.

# Chapters 24–25
# The Advocate; Postscript

## Summary

Ishmael interrupts his narrative to speak as an advocate for the dignity of the whaling industry and whales. He argues that whaling is a clean and upright profession that brings considerable profit to the economy. Whalers have expanded our understanding of the globe through exploration. The whale is important to world literature. Even kings and queens rely on whale oil for their coronations.

## Commentary

This is the first of more than forty chapters in which Ishmael halts the flow of the narrative to discuss some aspect of *cetology* (the study of whales), the whaling business, or the whale's reputation. Modern readers might well wonder why he does this. First, Ishmael tells us early on that he is going to sea to learn more of whales and whaling. He hopes to establish this as a worthwhile topic; that is why he refers to biblical sources such as the Book of Job or the Book of Jonah, here and throughout the novel, which add to the whale's reputation. Further enhancing the status of whales, he alludes to Alfred the Great (849–99 A.D, king of Wessex 871–99) who ended the Danish conquests in England; promoted English culture; *and*, Ishmael argues, wrote about whales. In addition, Melville grounds his story in *reality* by his sections on cetology. He wants to create at least the illusion of fact in the novel, and he does an admirable job of convincing the reader that these events could occur.

Finally, the reader should notice that the narrator is having a good time. For the most part, these chapters on cetology are not dull, dry, tedious accounts. The tone is light-hearted and sometimes even silly. In the chapter "Postscript," Ishmael argues that the whaling industry provides royalty with "coronation stuff" because the oil used to anoint a new king or queen probably is whale oil: "Think of that, ye loyal Britons!" avers the very American Ishmael.

Ishmael argues like a formal debater or a lawyer speaking to a jury, but his goal is to entertain as well as to inform. We might remember that Melville's audience in the 1850s consisted of more patient readers; they almost certainly had longer attention spans than we have today. A good book might last the winter, and Ishmael's wit would provide a welcomed break.

# Glossary

**superfluous** excessive, more than is needed.

**puissant** powerful.

**anoint** to put oil on in a ceremony of consecration.

# Chapters 26–27
# Knights and Squires

## Summary

Ishmael introduces some of the crew, beginning, in descending order under Ahab, with those in command. Chief mate is Starbuck, a thirty-year-old Quaker whose father and brother were killed in whaling accidents. Second mate is Stubb, "[g]ood-humored, easy, and careless," rarely seen awake without a pipe in his mouth. Third mate is Flask—short, stumpy, and pugnacious. Each will command an open boat when in pursuit of whales and have his own harpooner. The rest of the crew is a widely varied mix representing many parts of the world.

## Commentary

Literary
Device

One of Melville's consistent literary devices is the use of contrast. Here he employs it to distinguish character. The first mate is a devout Quaker, no hypocrite like the *Pequod*'s co-owner Bildad. He is calm, prudent, steady, and courageous, but he tempers his courage with a healthy respect for danger and an allowance for fear. As the novel progresses, Starbuck will contrast strikingly with Ahab, who is volatile, obsessed, wildly mad at times, and irreverent. Having first choice of harpooners, Starbuck takes Queequeg.

In a different light, Stubb and Flask also contrast with Starbuck and each other. Second mate Stubb is carefree, even careless. He loves a good joke and can be insensitive or deceitful, but he *is* a reliable seaman and whaler. Tashtego, an American Indian, will be his harpooner. Third mate Flask is stumpy and unattractive (while Starbuck is tall and handsome); more importantly, Flask lacks Starbuck's intelligence and elevation of character. The third mate is an adequate seaman but possesses none of Stubb's imagination or humor. Flask thinks whales are his personal enemies, contrasting with Starbuck who simply sees them as a means to a livelihood, but anticipating Ahab's more complicated hatred of Moby Dick. Flask's harpooner will be Daggoo, a huge (six feet, five inches tall) native of Africa. All the harpooners are especially proud men, understandably so because of their prestigious positions aboard ship.

Isolated as it is, and carrying a crew representing many parts of the globe, the *Pequod* serves as a microcosm of our planet. Ishmael observes that many of the crew are ignorant or even evil men, but he recognizes that each also has the capacity for exceptional valor, dignity, or democratic nobility. Most are not stereotypes; their virtues contrast with their vices just as they do in real people in the real world.

## Glossary

**squire** an attendant, especially to a medieval knight; here a reference to a harpooner.

**staid** sober, sedate, settled.

**steadfast** firm, fixed, established.

**pugnacious** combative, quarrelsome, ready for a fight.

**momentous** very important.

**august** here, imposing, magnificent, inspiring awe.

# Chapter 28

# Ahab

## Summary

After the *Pequod* has been at sea for several days, Ahab finally makes his first appearance. Ishmael tries to convince himself that Ahab has simply waited until the ship, sailing south, reached warmer climes. He describes the captain in emblematic ways. From that morning on, more is seen of Ahab.

## Commentary

Suspense is an effective literary device that Melville employs to develop an atmosphere of uncertainty or anticipation in the novel. The mystery surrounding Ahab and the voyage of the *Pequod* increases daily with Ahab's absence. Elijah's "diabolical" comments haunt Ishmael as he wonders about the captain and visually checks the rear of the ship, where the officer is quartered, whenever Ishmael is on duty. He tries to rationalize that Ahab is just waiting for warmer weather before he comes out of his cabin, but the captain's absence increases the narrator's sense of ominous concern.

When Ishmael finally does see Ahab standing on his quarter-deck one morning, "foreboding shivers" run over the crewman. He describes Ahab in emblematic terms that add to the mystery of the man. The language is especially effective here. The first we learn of the captain's appearance is that he does not seem to be ill but looks "like a man cut away from the stake, when the fire has overrunningly wasted all the limbs without consuming them." Next we are told that Ahab looks like a sculpture of solid bronze; he is compared to an oak or some other sort of great tree. The captain has a prominent scar, "lividly whitish," running from the top of his head down his face and neck until it disappears beneath his clothing. It is compared to the mark of a lightning bolt, and an old Indian on board claims that it runs the length of Ahab's body, "crown to sole"; we get the feeling that a lightning bolt pierced this "grand, ungodly, god-like man" (Chapter 16) to his very *soul.* There is a grim look on the captain's face, "an infinity of firmest fortitude, a determinate, unsurrenderable" willfulness in his visage. This is all so overpowering that it takes Ishmael a few seconds to notice the leg—a barbaric, white, ivory prosthesis "fashioned from the polished bone of the sperm whale's jaw." The lower tip of the artificial leg is anchored in a hole in the quarter-deck, apparently bored for that purpose. (There is another such hole on the other side of the ship.) The description indicates a man larger than life; touched by heaven's bolt, for good or evil; and partly carved from a sperm whale's jaw.

## Glossary

**peremptory** final, absolute, decisive.

**vicariously** on behalf of another.

**watch** any of the periods of duty into which work is divided onboard ship.

**Cellini** Benvenuto Cellini (1500–71), Italian sculptor also known for his autobiography.

**mizzen shrouds** the ropes connecting the third mast (from the front) to the ship's sides.

**auger** a narrow tool for boring holes in wood.

## Chapters 29–31

# Enter Ahab: To Him, Stubb; The Pipe; Queen Mab

## Summary

Ahab spends less and less time in his cabin. "It feels like going down into one's tomb," he is heard to mutter. His nightly pacing on deck, his whale-jaw leg thumping, disturbs some of the crew below. When Stubb humorously asks the captain if the noise might be muffled, Ahab calls the second mate a dog and ten times a donkey, dismissing him. Ahab finds no comfort in a smoke and hurls his lighted pipe into the sea. Stubb has a disturbing dream.

## Commentary

These chapters cast further illumination on the character of Ahab. As the *Pequod* sails farther south and nears the area where whales might be found, its captain grows increasingly restless. His habit of walking the deck at night is particularly disturbing to some of the crew who are trying to sleep below. Stubb's cautious, good-natured attempt to have the captain somehow muffle the constant thumping of his artificial leg is met with hostility from Ahab. Aboard a whaler in the mid-nineteenth century, Ishmael points out, the captain is king.

We see further into Ahab's troubled soul after Stubb is dismissed. Lighting his pipe by the binnacle lamp, the captain sits for an apparent moment of serenity; his mind, however, takes no pleasure in peaceful contemplation. It is driven toward a single goal. He casts the pipe into the waters as brusquely as he dismissed Stubb and resumes his pacing on the planks.

We also learn more of Stubb. In addition to the biblical Ten Commandments (Exodus 20:2–17; Deuteronomy 5:6–22), Stubb has an eleventh ("Think not") and a twelfth ("Sleep when you can"). But this night, sleep brings no respite to Stubb. He dreams that Ahab kicks him with the old man's ivory leg. When Stubb kicks back, the second mate's leg flies off. Ahab suddenly turns into a pyramid; as Stubb kicks at that, a hunchbacked "badger-haired old merman" calls him to desist and says that it's an honor to be kicked by a man as wise as Ahab. Like most of the rest of the crew, Stubb is confused and troubled by his captain's behavior; but he is also drawn to the monomaniacal commander, respects him, sees him as a great man, and will follow Ahab anywhere.

## Glossary

**aught** to any degree.

**binnacle** an upright, cylindrical stand holding the ship's compass.

**Queen Mab** in folklore, a fairy queen who controls people's dreams.

**monomaniacal** irrationally preoccupied with one subject.

## Chapters 32–35

# Cetology; The Specksynder; The Cabin-Table; The Mast-Head

## Summary

In one of many considerations of cetology (the study of whales), Ishmael tells us of various types of leviathan, of which he values the sperm whale most highly. His attention then shifts to life aboard ship as he discusses the chain of command and some of the ways in which this hierarchy is demonstrated in daily life. The narrator considers the beauties and dangers of serving watch at the masthead.

## Commentary

Melville breaks the intensity of Ahab's introduction with these informative chapters in which Ishmael considers types of whales as well as life aboard ship.

Ishmael's discussion of the hierarchy of whales demonstrates his pride in, and the importance he places on, whaling. He has deepest admiration for the sperm whale. It is, he says, the largest denizen of the globe and the most formidable to encounter, earning any experienced whaler's respect. More important to the whaling business, it is also the most valuable type of whale because it is the leading source of spermaceti, a white, wax-like substance taken from the oil in the head and used to make cosmetics, ointments, and candles. To Ishmael, the sperm whale is a noble creature, adding significance to the business of whaling but also to Ahab's quest, of which we are just beginning to be informed.

A whaling vessel also has a kind of hierarchy, a chain of command that is essential to discipline and efficiency. Its effect can be seen in the daily lives of the men aboard. The crew on a whaler is quartered at the front of the vessel; the captain, mates, *and* harpooners sleep at the back of the ship. Of special interest is the respect shown the harpooners. Their backgrounds may be primitive, as is the case on this voyage, but they are treated like a class of officers because of the importance of their unique skills. In the old days, two hundred years before our story, authority aboard Dutch whalers was divided between the regular naval captain and a "Specksynder"—literally, a "Fat-Cutter," but in fact the chief harpooner who controlled the whale hunt. While this office no longer exists in the industry of Ishmael's time, dominated by Americans, harpooners are quartered with the officers, eat at the captain's table *after* the other officers have finished, and receive considerable respect.

Whaling is dangerous for all aboard, especially those posted to watch for whales in the masthead, the highest point on the ship. While the view can be awe-inspiring on a beautiful day, merely climbing to the masthead is dangerous. Nor is this perch on a southern whaler, such as the *Pequod*, a protected "crow's nest" as one might find on a ship in northern waters. It is an open perch with bars for holding on but no protection. When rough weather hits, the hapless sailor on masthead watch must fend for himself.

# Glossary

**penem . . . lactantem; ex lege . . . meritoque** Latin, "a penis that enters the female that suckles from breasts; from the law of nature with justice and merit." The narrator quotes this scholarly definition of a mammal for the purpose of ironic humor. He thinks a whale is a fish either way.

**abridged** condensed, shortened but keeping the main contents.

**hustings** a deliberative assembly; here, politics, a political campaign.

**saline** salty.

**progeny** descendants, offspring.

**abstemious** characterized by abstinence.

**buckler** a small, round shield held by hand or worn on the arm.

## Chapter 36

# The Quarter-Deck

## Summary

A few days after the incident with his pipe, Ahab spends a restless day in his cabin or pacing the quarter-deck. Near the end of the day, he issues an unusual order: The entire crew, even the masthead watch, is to assemble before him. Ahab briefly discusses procedure for announcing the sighting of a whale and offers a Spanish ounce of gold to the first man to spot the White Whale. He enlists the crew's support in a mission to kill Moby Dick; only Starbuck objects. Ahab and the crew celebrate.

## Commentary

In one of the most significant chapters in the novel, Melville employs a dramatic technique—complete with brief stage directions, dialogue, and rousing speech, as well as narrative intervention. This is one of several dramatized chapters in the novel. The method is especially effective here because it allows the reader to see how charismatic and forceful Ahab can be as a leader and speaker.

Style & Language

As the day wears on, it is clear to Stubb that something important is stirring in Ahab. The second mate tells Flask that "the chick that's in him [Ahab] pecks the shell." This is the time that Ahab chooses to announce his true intentions to the crew and attempt to persuade the men to join him in a singular effort to hunt down the White Whale. Like a speaker at a political rally, Ahab first unifies the group by asking a series of emotionally charged questions that call for unified responses: What do you do when you spot a whale? What do you do next? What tune do you pull to in pursuit? The men are increasingly excited, almost as if they are in the blood lust of a real hunt. Ahab then employs his prop, a Spanish gold ounce, offered to the man who first sees ("raises") the White Whale. He dramatically holds up the coin to the declining sun and nails it to the mainmast.

The harpooners are the first to recognize the whale's description—the white head, wrinkled brow, crooked jaw, three holes in the starboard fluke—as that of Moby Dick. Their enthusiastic confirmations, and the revelation that Moby Dick took off the captain's leg, lead Ahab into an emotional appeal to the crew to join him in chasing the whale "over all sides of earth, till he spouts black blood and rolls fin out." The men shout their enthusiastic approval. The only abstention is from Starbuck who wants to stick to the business of accumulating whale oil and thinks it "blasphemous" to seek revenge on a "dumb brute—that simply smote thee from blindest instinct!" Ahab responds that he would "strike the sun if it insulted me." This scene clarifies the primary difference between Starbuck and Ahab: Starbuck attributes no meaning to how and why things happen; Ahab interprets meaning in everything.

**Character Insight**

Scholars dispute whether Ahab considers Moby Dick to be a representative of evil or whether the captain's vanity is so great that he wants to take on the structure of nature, even God himself. Is the whale evil, or is the evil in Ahab? The captain seems half-mad as he rants about attacking the "inscrutable thing" behind the "mask," the force behind the façade that is the whale. To understand Ahab's obsession, we must try to understand what he really wants to kill. Is it the whale or a power he sees behind the whale? These are questions to consider as the novel progresses. A convincing argument can be made that Ahab wants to *be* God and is offended that he should have to bear the insult of any authority beyond himself. The "inscrutable thing" dares to limit Ahab's role in the world. Ahab thinks that he is filled with a superhuman power, an interior electricity that would kill mere mortals. As he offers wine to the three harpooners, ceremonially celebrating a commitment to a unified cause, the scene has the impact of a diabolical black mass. Ahab is a powerful man, charismatic, obsessed, even mad, and he has all but one of the crew under his control.

## Glossary

**perdition** damnation, Hell.

**inscrutable** obscure, mysterious, enigmatic.

**tacit** unspoken.

## Chapters 37–40

# Sunset; Dusk; First Night-Watch; Midnight, Forecastle

## Summary

As evening turns into night, various characters react to the events of the day. At sunset, Ahab, in his cabin, is pleased with the ease with which he swayed the crew and is outspoken in his determination. At dusk by the mainmast, Starbuck feels incapable of changing his captain's plan and is resigned to his role. At the night's first watch (8 p.m.) atop the foremast (nearest the front of the ship), Stubb's reaction is to laugh at the absurdity of it all. At midnight, in the forecastle some of the crew and harpooners are still partying and drinking wine.

## Commentary

In these chapters, Melville continues to present dramatic scenes, using brief stage directions, soliloquy, and dialogue. There is no narration from Ishmael. In addition to progressing the plot, Melville is able to offer the reader character insights through the thoughts and speech of Ahab, Starbuck, Stubb, and assorted crewmen.

Through his cabin windows at the back of the ship, Ahab can see the "white and turbid wake" of the ship's passing and thinks of it as his own momentous impress on the world. His vanity includes an apparent pride in being what he calls "demoniac"; as he says, he is "madness maddened!" He mocks the gods and is determined to be both the prophet of his revenge and its executioner.

**Character Insight**

Starbuck's response contrasts with most of the crew's in a revealing way. The first mate recognizes that he is no match for his captain and is resigned to Ahab's "Heaven-insulting purpose"; yet he fears the ominous future. Stubb typically tries to laugh at the "predestinated" situation and sings a drinking song. Most of the rest of the crew, representing various parts of the world, are content to party past midnight; they seem oblivious to their journey into doom. An exception is young Pip, the cabin servant who finds terror where the rest see cause for "jollies." We will learn more about his insights in Chapter 93.

## Glossary

**turbid** thick, dense, and dark.

**whelp** a puppy or cub.

**eight bells** here, midnight, the end of the watch that began at 8 p.m. The ringing of a bell marks each half hour of the watch.

## Chapters 41–42

# Moby Dick; The Whiteness of the Whale

## Summary

Ishmael returns as narrator to tell us what he has heard of the White Whale. Because his information is all hearsay—something he has heard from others but cannot yet prove—he concedes that much of it may be exaggerated. In fact, Moby Dick has already become a sort of legendary figure, reputedly omnipresent (he supposedly appears at different places at the same time) and perhaps immortal and eternal, which Ishmael explains as being omnipresent in time. We learn more details of Ahab's loss of leg, and Ishmael considers the meaning of "whiteness."

## Commentary

Having presented Ahab's proposal and the crew's reaction in dramatic form, Melville returns the telling of the story to Ishmael. The narrator admits that he, like most of the crew, was overpowered by Ahab's charismatic appeal, although Ishmael anticipates the rest of the voyage with dread in his soul.

**Character Insight**

We already know a fair amount about the White Whale, which we might think of as a key *character* in the novel. In these two chapters, Ishmael expands on its physical description and considers reports that range from likely to fanciful. From Ahab and the harpooners (Chapter 36), and now from Ishmael, we learn that Moby Dick is an exceptionally large *sperm* whale with a snow-white head, a wrinkled brow, a crooked jaw, an especially bushy spout, and three holes in the right fluke of his tail. His hump is also white and shaped like a pyramid. The rest of his body is marbled with white. He fantails oddly before he submerges. One of Moby Dick's favorite tricks is to seem to be fleeing but suddenly turn on his pursuers and destroy their open boats. Sailors attribute great intelligence and malignity to the White Whale.

What is the White Whale to Ahab? Ishmael thinks that Ahab views the whale as an embodiment of all evil. It may be helpful to consider Ahab's comments in Chapter 36. The irrepressible captain there sees Moby Dick as a "mask," behind which lies a great power whose dominance Ahab refuses to accept. Ahab himself says (Chapter 41) that his means are sane but his motive and object are mad. However, Ahab may not be the best judge. We are told that he was attacking the White Whale with only a six-inch blade, like an "Arkansas duellist," the day that Moby Dick's lower teeth sliced away the captain's leg as a mower would a blade of grass. *That* method of attacking the whale seems insane, driven by the captain's excessive determination.

Many scholars, including most notably Harold Bloom (in *Moby-Dick: Modern Critical Interpretations*) consider Chapter 42, "The Whiteness of the Whale," to be the "visionary center" of the novel and perhaps of all of Melville's writing. Students might note the rich ambiguity of Ishmael's inquiry into the significance of the whale's "visible absence of color." In that whiteness, Ishmael sees innocence and evil, glory and damnation in a nine-page chapter that is one of the most rewarding in the novel. We are not spoon-fed meaning by Melville. As with most great writers, he allows the reader to form his own conclusions. Ahab appears to be a great man but a madman; but what is Moby Dick?

## Glossary

**malignity**  intense ill will, a quality of being harmful or dangerous.

**erudite**  having or showing great knowledge gained from reading.

**ubiquitous**  seeming to be present everywhere at the same time.

**fathom**  six feet, a unit of length used to measure the depth of water or the length of nautical rope or cable.

**legerdemain**  sleight of hand, tricks of a stage magician.

## Chapters 43–45

# Hark!; The Chart; The Affidavit

## Summary

One quiet night while working near the rear of the ship, one of the seamen hears a mysterious sound, perhaps a human cough, beneath the hatches of a part of the ship where the crew never is allowed. The source of the sound remains unidentified. Meanwhile, Ahab spends his evenings poring over charts of the world's oceans, searching for patterns in the movement of whales. Ishmael feels it is time to swear certain facts to the reader so that we might believe the story that he is telling us.

## Commentary

Some of the mystery of the voyage is still unexplained. What were those shapes that Ishmael thought he saw entering the boat on Christmas morning? Are they related to the strange sounds heard below the hatches near the captain's quarters? Ahab may know, but he is not talking. The captain spends most evenings trying to guess where Moby Dick might be. Ishmael assures us that whales do migrate in certain patterns, but the sperm whale's routes vary more than most, and it's a big world.

In Chapter 45, Ishmael attempts to convince the reader that the story he tells is consistent with possibility. As if he were swearing an oath, Ishmael reveals that Ahab is justified in believing that his own harpoons still ride Moby Dick and that he may well be the one to kill the White Whale; such odd things have happened. Nor is it unique that Moby Dick is recognizable; so are several other sperm whales, some given names. Foreshadowing events later in the novel, Ishmael warns that hunting whales in an open boat is very dangerous and that sperm whales have even been known to attack and sink large ships. Ishmael is concerned that, without these "plain facts, historical and otherwise," the reader "might scout at Moby Dick as a monstrous fable" or, worse, an allegory. He asks us to suspend our disbelief, we must suspect, *because* this is a grand, mythic journey with so many tempting, hidden meanings. Ishmael asks us to stick to the story.

# Glossary

**scuttle-butt** a container for drinking-water aboard ship; information passed at such a place.

**ratification** approval or confirmation.

**affidavit** a written statement made under oath.

**facetiousness** joking or trying to be amusing.

**Saul of Tarsus** original name of the biblical Apostle to the Gentiles, Saint Paul.

## Chapters 46–49
# Surmises; The Mat-Maker; The First Lowering; The Hyena

## Summary

Ishmael speculates on Ahab's motivation for continuing to look for whales other than Moby Dick. As Queequeg and Ishmael work on a mat to lash to the boat, Tashtego spots a school of sperm whales and sounds the alarm, "There she blows!" Almost immediately, the men spring into action and begin lowering boats. Suddenly, "five dusky phantoms" surround Ahab. Ishmael's boat is swamped in the ensuing whale chase, but all aboard escape with their lives.

## Commentary

Character Insight

Ishmael offers further insight into the captain's character as he surmises that Ahab may continue to seek other whales because it is in his "fiery whaleman's" nature or because he resents all whales. More likely, he suggests, Ahab realizes that his men need short-term goals and are interested in pursuits that will fill their purses. They also need some practice. As a wise leader, he encourages the hunt. Ahab is also a very private man who tells the crew only what he thinks it should know. The mystery of the shadowy figures (on Christmas morning) and the sounds below deck are solved when five "aboriginal natives of the Manillas" suddenly surround the captain at the first lowering. A whaling captain usually stays aboard ship during the actual hunt; during this voyage, Ahab will join the chase with the aborigines as his crew. Their leader is a white-turbaned old man named Fedallah, of whom we will hear more later. There is a continuing aura of secrecy and perhaps even evil about the aborigines. Ishmael points out that some white mariners believe that natives of the Manillas are "paid spies and secret confidential agents on the water of the devil, their lord."

Ishmael has previously discussed the dangers of pursuing whales in an open boat; here they are demonstrated. Chapter 48 is an exciting account of an unsuccessful whale chase, culminating in the loss of Starbuck's boat on which Ishmael is part of that day's crew. Ishmael is amazed at the other men's light-hearted response to this near-death experience. When he returns to the ship, he promptly draws his will.

# Glossary

**surmises** conjectures, speculations, guesses.

**impunity** exemption from punishment, penalty, or harm.

**ostentatious** showy, pretentious.

**inscrutable** difficult to understand, mysterious.

**cataract** a large waterfall or deluge that is difficult to see through.

## Chapters 50–51

# Ahab's Boat and Crew: Fedallah; The Spirit-Spout

## Summary

Without the owners' knowledge, Ahab has brought aboard his own private crew of four oarsmen and the harpooner Fedallah. Except for Fedallah, their mystery soon fades; the *Pequod* crew works with and accepts the aborigines as able seamen. Weeks pass, and the ship approaches the southern tip of Africa. On a moonlit night, Fedallah spots a silvery spout in the distance.

## Commentary

**Character Insight**

These chapters provide further insight into the character of Fedallah, who still remains an inscrutable figure. He moves about like a phantom and seems to have an odd influence over Ahab. Ishmael compares him to a type of ancient, ghostlike figure, which one might find among the unchanging Asian communities. He may even be a demon.

The silvery spout, which Fedallah first spots in the distance while standing mainmast watch at night, adds to the mysterious atmosphere. Try as it might, the *Pequod* can never catch up to it. Sometimes it disappears for days at a time. The vision, if that's what it is, seems to appear and vanish at will, repeatedly, but is seen only at night. Some of the men claim that it is Moby Dick—taunting, luring, beckoning them to follow, again and again, until the White Whale can at last turn and destroy them. Rounding the Cape of Good Hope, at the southern tip of Africa, the ship finally loses the silvery specter, which is replaced by very real winds and rough seas.

## Glossary

**vicissitude** a condition of constant change or alternation, mutability.

**Beelzebub** a chief devil; sometimes used for Satan.

**yaw** to swing back and forth across its course, as a ship hit by high waves.

**repugnance** extreme dislike or distaste, aversion.

**perfidious** dishonest, betraying, treacherous.

## Chapters 52–54

# The *Albatross*; The Gam; The *Town-Ho*'s Story

## Summary

Ishmael defines "gam" and comments on the *Pequod*'s first two gams of this voyage. The initial opportunity for communication with another ship is aborted when the captain of the *Albatross* drops his speaking trumpet in strong winds. The second ship, the *Town-Ho*, oddly features a crew that consists, primarily, of Polynesians. There is a long story behind this, and Ishmael delights in telling all the details.

## Commentary

We learn more about sailing customs of the time in these chapters. Of equal interest are the continuing insights into the characters of Ahab and Ishmael. But first we must understand the definition of a "gam."

In the chapter of that name, Ishmael explains that a *gam* is a "social meeting of two (or more) ships, generally on a cruising ground." The crews visit each other, the two captains on one ship and the chief mates on the other. Newspapers might be passed from the ship most recently in port. Likewise, the outward-bound vessel might have letters for some of the other ship's crew. In exchange, the ship longer at sea reports its sightings of whales. The area around the Cape of Good Hope is populated by more ships than any other similar region in the world, we are told, and the American whalers especially enjoy a good gam. An exception is Ahab who is interested only in the answer to one question: "Hast seen the White Whale?" The *Pequod* meets several other whalers on its journey halfway around the world; the monomaniacal Ahab has only the one interest in each. But he does allow a gam with the *Town-Ho*, which *has* seen the whale.

Ishmael enjoys repeating the *Town-Ho*'s story just as he once told it, he says, to a group of "Spanish friends" at the Golden Inn at Lima, Peru. This allows two interesting insights regarding Ishmael. First, it offers further evidence that the narrator survives the novel; he lives to tell the tale of *Moby-Dick* as well as the story at the Golden Inn. In addition, we see in the Golden Inn an Ishmael who is much more mature, experienced, and sure of himself than the rookie whaling sailor who is on the *Pequod*.

**Literary Device**

The story itself is a yarn within a yarn, told within the framework of the novel, involving a crisis at sea for the *Town-Ho*. During its current journey, the ship sprung a leak. In an attempt to keep it afloat, the crew was driven unreasonably. Suddenly Moby Dick appeared. Being stalwart whaling men, the crew took after the White Whale but harvested only disaster. A nice touch in Ishmael's story telling occurs when Moby Dick rises to expose a bit of the red woolen shirt of one of his victims, stuck between the White Whale's teeth like a bit of tomato. Most of the crew survived the episode with the White Whale but abandoned ship and were replaced at a nearby island: thus the mostly Polynesian crew.

## Glossary

**Albatross** a large, web-footed bird found chiefly in the South Seas; a burden (see Samuel Taylor Coleridge's "The Rime of the Ancient Mariner," 1798).

**ostensible** apparent.

**brace of dandies** a pair of fops, men who pay too much attention to appearance.

**ballast** anything heavy carried in a ship to give stability.

**fetid** decaying, putrid, having a bad smell.

## Chapters 55–60

# Of the Monstrous Pictures of Whales; Of the Less Erroneous Pictures of Whales and the True Pictures of Whaling Scenes; Of Whales in Paint, in Teeth, in Sheet-Iron, in Stone, in Mountains, in Stars; Brit; Squid; The Line

## Summary

Ishmael considers assorted depictions of whales in art, disapproving of most but conceding that some are more nearly accurate. Returning to the story, the *Pequod* comes upon "vast meadows of brit," upon which the right whale feeds. As the ship heads for Java, Daggoo, on watch, spots a great white mass in the distance and cries out that it is the White Whale. It turns out to be a giant squid. Ishmael discusses the strength and usage of the whale line in open boats.

## Commentary

Ishmael is annoyed by the inaccurate manner in which whales and whaling are depicted in art. He recommends "going a whaling" yourself if you seek even "a tolerable idea of his [the whale's] living contour." Of course, that can be a dangerous venture, resulting in one's death, so perhaps it is best to leave it alone. Only a couple of French engravings come close to depicting the whale and whaling scenes accurately, according to Ishmael. He also respects the paintings of an artist he calls Garnery (Louis Garneray, 1783–1857; the mistaken spelling may be intentional, to add authenticity to Ishmael's riff; he claims not to know who the then-famous artist is). He has seen many "lively" examples of "skrimshander" (scrimshaw), intricate carvings made by sailors on whalebones or other surfaces.

Ishmael informs us further of life at sea. He considers the ecology of the ocean as he discusses vast areas of brit, a minute, yellow substance that collectively looks like "fields of ripe and golden wheat." The scene is peaceful enough as the right whales feed on the brit, reminding Ishmael of mowers cutting a meadow. But there is also a terrible violence in the sea. Creatures feed upon each other, and even the great sperm whale is subject to a cruel fate from nature or man. Again Ishmael warns that the ocean is an especially dangerous place for people.

**Literary Device**

The chapter on the line, or rope, returns to an immediate consideration of the whaling industry. Manila ropes are only two-thirds of an inch thick, but they are amazingly strong, due to their quality and tight weave, and "bear a strain nearly equal to three tons," the narrator tells us. On one end is secured a harpoon. During the hunt, the rope is carried coiled in a tub on the open boat. The lower end is free but can be linked to another boat's line if the whale "sounds" (dives deep underwater); or it can be secured to the boat so that a fleeing whale carries the boat with it. With even a slight error, the line can take a sailor's arm, leg, head, or entire body with it, which foreshadows a key event at the end of the novel.

# Glossary

**extant** still existing, not extinct.

**Vishnu** in Hinduism, the second member of the trinity, called "the Preserver."

**frigate** a fast, medium-sized, sailing warship.

**furlong** a unit of measure equal to an eighth of a mile or 220 yards.

## Chapters 61–66

# Stubb Kills a Whale; The Dart; The Crotch; Stubb's Supper; The Whale as a Dish; The Shark Massacre

## Summary

In these chapters, Ishmael gives an account of a successful hunt and its immediate aftermath. Spotting a large sperm whale about 100 yards from the boat, the crew springs into action. Stubb's boat makes the kill, and the second mate celebrates with a whale steak for supper. Stubb harasses Fleece, the African-American cook, and prods him into delivering a sermon to sharks who are attacking the whale carcass.

## Commentary

Melville uses idiomatic dialogue to provide character insight in this section of the novel. This is part of a realistic portrayal of a successful whale hunt, but a modern audience may question the effect. It begins with Queequeg, from whom we have not heard much since the ship set sail. Some of the men believe that the giant white squid was an omen of bad luck, but Queequeg takes a practical approach reflecting his considerable experience as a harpooner: "When you see him 'quid,' . . . then you quick see him 'parm whale." He is correct; the sperm whale soon appears.

Stubb is an able seaman but a coarse prankster. After making the kill, he calls for the black cook, Fleece, to prepare a steak in celebration. Nothing that Fleece does seems to be satisfactory. Stubb apparently thinks of himself as quite a wit and superior to Fleece in every way as he summons the chef: "Cook, cook!—where's that old Fleece? . . . cook, you cook!—sail this way, cook!" Stubb complains that the whale steak, though reddish, is too well done and tender; he wants it tough! In addition, he can barely hear himself yell at Fleece because the sharks are making so much noise; he orders Fleece to deliver them a sermon. Fleece speaks in the stereotypical dialect too often assigned to African Americans in the literature of the day. Preaching to the sharks, he says, "Stop dat dam smackin' ob de lips! Massa Stubb say dat you can fill your dam bellies up de hatchings, but by Gor! you must stop dat dam racket!"

Perhaps we should remember that it is Stubb doing the harassing, not Ishmael or Melville. However, there are no repercussions for the second mate's abusive badgering. The publication date of the novel was 1851, almost a dozen years before the Emancipation Proclamation, which technically, if not yet effectively, ended slavery in the United States and its territories. The extended scene between Stubb and Fleece probably is supposed to be funny.

## Glossary

**The Crotch** a notched, perpendicular stick that holds two harpoons for quick accessibility.

**audacious** bold or daring.

**elucidate** to make clear, to explain.

**unctuous** oily, greasy; smug, smoothly pretentious.

## Chapters 67–70

# Cutting In; The Blanket; The Funeral; The Sphynx

## Summary

The account of the aftermath of the hunt continues as the crew uses blocks and tackles, harpoons, and other slicing devices to harvest the "blanket" of blubber from the whale. The whale's head is removed because that is where the valuable spermaceti can be found. With a small whale, the head might be taken aboard; with one as large as this day's kill, the head is only lifted partially out of the water and worked on from above, at the side of the ship. Ishmael compares the abandoning of the carcass to a funeral.

## Commentary

The tone of these chapters is objective and businesslike, broken by a further insight into the characters of Ishmael and Ahab. The whalers are professionally interested in two things: the "blanket" of fat that forms the skin of the whale; and its head, which contains the most valuable product. The whale's blubber runs as much as fifteen inches thick and is peeled like an orange's skin. It is boiled to render the oil—about ten barrels of oil to the ton, a hundred barrels with a very large sperm whale.

When the carcass is released, Ishmael watches it float away and sees this as a doleful and mocking funeral. He compares the sea vultures, which prepare to feed on the carcass, to "air-sharks," representative of the predatory cruelty of life, especially life at sea. Ishmael is a poet-philosopher, as is Ahab, which partially explains Ishmael's deep interest in the captain.

The head of the whale is very valuable because that is where the white, wax-like spermaceti is found. The decapitated head, which constitutes a third of the leviathan's bulk, is cumbersome but necessary to the industry. Ishmael will return to this topic in Chapters 74–80.

**Character Insight**

Revealingly, to Ahab the head looks more like a mysterious sphinx than a source of revenue. He wonders what secrets the head could tell since it has been where "unrecorded names and navies rust" and has "slept by many a sailor's side, where sleepless mothers would give their lives to lay them down." Ahab is a complicated man. His flaws *and* his virtues are huge. It would be a mistake to dismiss him or to try to categorize him simply.

## Glossary

**ex officio**  Latin, "by virtue of one's office or position."

**insatiate**  never satisfied.

**punctilious**  very careful about every detail.

# Chapter 71
# The *Jeroboam's* Story

## Summary

As the *Pequod's* crew works on the whale, another Nantucket whaling ship, named the *Jeroboam*, approaches. Its captain and some of the crew come nearby in an open boat. There is a "malignant epidemic" aboard the *Jeroboam* so the captain refuses to board Ahab's vessel. In addition, the stranger ship seems almost under the control of a raving Shaker prophet who thinks he is the archangel Gabriel. Gabriel believes that Moby Dick is the incarnation of the Shaker God and warns against confronting the White Whale.

## Commentary

Style & Language

The meeting with the *Jeroboam* heightens the ominous atmosphere surrounding the *Pequod's* quest. It is important to note that the biblical Jeroboam (1 Kings 11–14) suffers because of obstinacy and his failure to heed the warnings of a prophet. So, too, the vessel *Jeroboam* suffers when it ignores Gabriel, mad though this Gabriel may be. (The biblical Gabriel [Daniel 8:16; Luke 1:26] is a herald of *good* news, including, to Mary, the revelation that she will be the mother of Christ.)

In the novel, Gabriel warns against confronting Moby Dick who is, he claims, the Shaker God; this adds to the mystery of what Moby Dick really is. When the *Jeroboam's* crew did pursue the White Whale, one of its mates, Harry Macey, was killed in a mysterious way as the whale's sweeping tail hit only him, leaving the open boat and the rest of its crew untouched. Gabriel also claims to have caused the "plague" aboard ship and to be the only source of its cure.

As the *Jeroboam* and the *Pequod* attempt their awkward, quarantined gam, Ahab remembers that he has a letter for the deceased Macey and tries to pass it to the other ship's captain. Gabriel grabs the letter and casts it back aboard the *Pequod*, crying, "Nay, keep it thyself, . . . thou art soon going that way," meaning that Ahab will soon join Macey at the bottom of the sea.

## Glossary

**Shakers** here, short for Shaking Quakers, a sect so named because of trembling caused by emotional stress or euphoria of devotions.

**bilious** bad-tempered, cross.

## Chapters 72–73

# The Monkey-Rope; Stubb and Flask Kill a Right Whale and Then Have a Talk over Him

## Summary

In order to attach the blubber hook to a captured whale, a harpooner is lowered to the leviathan's back as it lies nearly submerged alongside the ship. In this precarious position, the harpooner's safety relies on his attachment, by a "monkey-rope," to a crewman on deck. Flask explains to Stubb the reason for hunting a right whale, whose oil is inferior.

## Commentary

Theme

The theme of friendship is renewed in Chapter 72 as Queequeg and Ishmael are together again. The harpooner is lowered, off the side of the ship, onto the back of a dangerously bobbing whale carcass in order to attach a heavy, awkward blubber hook. Often the harpooner must remain in that dangerous position for some time as the stripping of fat proceeds. To keep him from falling off, into the jaws of ravenous sharks, the harpooner is attached to his *bowsman,* the man who pulls the second oar from forward in his boat, by a line called a "monkey-rope." In this case, the harpooner and bowsman are Queequeg and Ishmael. The monkey-rope seems to symbolize their friendship and the links among mankind that help us to survive.

Superstition often plays a role aboard the whaler. An example is the killing and securing of a right whale by Stubb and Flask. The second mate wonders why Ahab would want the inferior oil of a right whale. Flask is surprised that Stubb has not heard that a ship with a sperm whale's head lashed to its starboard (right while facing forward) side, as is the case currently with the *Pequod,* and a right whale's head lashed to the larboard (left, port), supposedly cannot capsize.

## Glossary

**Siamese** joined, as with Siamese twins.

**maw** here, the throat, gullet, or jaws of a voracious animal or fish.

**apothecary** a pharmacist or druggist.

**prodigious** of great size or power.

## Chapters 74–80

# The Sperm Whale's Head— Contrasted View; The Right Whale's Head—Contrasted View; The Battering Ram; The Great Heidelburgh Tun; Cistern and Buckets; The Prairie; The Nut

## Summary

Ishmael compares the heads of the sperm and right whales. He sees the sperm whale's forehead as an extremely efficient battering ram while the massive tun of oil in the sperm whale's head reminds him of the Heidelberg Castle wine cask, which has a capacity of 49,000 gallons. Tashtego falls into the whale's head and is rescued by Queequeg. The sperm whale's brain is relatively small, only a "nut."

## Commentary

Character Insight

Ishmael returns to one of his favorite topics, cetology, as he compares the two heads that are attached to the sides of the ship. Throughout the book, the narrator seems to thrive on contrasts: good vs. evil, white vs. black, starboard vs. port, God vs. Satan, madness vs. reason. However, it must be said that Ishmael seldom actually *sees* the world in such simplistic terms. Ultimately, opposites are only philosophical points of departure for the narrator. Neither Ahab nor Moby Dick, for example, can be limited to a single definition. The characters and issues here are complex, and Ishmael seems to delight in that rich view of life.

In these chapters, Ishmael's starting place is the contrast between the heads of the sperm and right whales. These are the only types of whale hunted by man, he tells us. Of the two, Ishmael feels that the sperm has more character; it is also much more valuable commercially. Its forehead is the world's most efficient natural battering ram, foreshadowing events at the end of the novel. The whale's eyes are small, reminding Ishmael of a colt's but lashless; they are placed on either side of the head so that the leviathan must get two distinct pictures of the world simultaneously, an ocular dichotomy that fits Ishmael's own initial view of life. He wonders how the *whale* blends the two outlooks. The ears are tiny, barely large enough to hold a writing quill. The sperm's ears have an outside opening; the right whale's ears are covered with a membrane.

**Literary Device**

Chapter 78 features an interesting literary device. Before long, it is apparent that Ishmael is more interested in the sperm whale. He enjoys the unique fact that the sperm's head can carry up to 500 gallons of valuable spermaceti oil. The image of Tashtego nearly drowning in it, rescued only by Queequeg, is an instance in which Melville uses dramatic action to illustrate a cetological point. It also breaks the monotony of what could be an excessively dry topic.

## Glossary

**vacillate**  to sway to and fro, to waver in mind.

**shoemaker's last**  a block or form shaped like a person's foot and used for making or repairing shoes.

**for the nonce**  for the time being.

**volition**  the act of using the will, a deliberate decision.

**prairie**  a type of clam, here compared to the whale's head.

**citadel**  a fortress, usually on a commanding height.

# Chapter 81

# The *Pequod* Meets the *Virgin*

## Summary

Continuing with its voyage, the *Pequod* soon comes across the German whaler *Jungfrau*, Derick De Deer captain. The *Jungfrau* has had no success hunting whales and desperately needs to procure some oil for its own use. It has not encountered the White Whale. Ahab is disappointed but supplies the oil. Before Captain Derick can return to his ship, a pod of whales is sighted. Both crews give chase with disappointing results. The *Jungfrau* crew chases a fin-back.

## Commentary

The gams that the *Pequod* encounters are usually frustrating or otherwise disappointing. Ahab is interested only in information regarding Moby Dick. When the other ship has not encountered the White Whale, or its captain wants to discuss something else, Ahab prefers to move on as soon as possible. Communication is even more strained than usual with the *Jungfrau* because of the language barrier, which some critics see as symbolic of the difficulty involved in a visitor's attempt at any conversation with Ahab.

*Jungfrau* is German for "young woman," which Melville translates as "virgin." The ship is a virgin in the sense that it is inexperienced. It is, Ishmael tells us, "clean"—that is, it is empty of oil and has not yet secured its first whale. The captain and crew of the German vessel are woefully inexperienced at whaling. Ahab's men easily beat the Germans to the one whale in the pod that is captured, although the sperm whale seems sickly and soon sinks to the bottom of the ocean. The Germans then naively take after a fin-back whale, which a novice might confuse with a sperm because the spouts are similar. Veteran whalers do not pursue the fin-back because it is too swift to be caught. Ahab's experienced men desist. Captain Derick encourages pursuit. At the end of the chapter, Ishmael offers one of his universal observations, inferred from the specific situation, as he comments on the futile chase: "Oh! many are the Fin-Backs, and many are the Dericks, my friend."

# Glossary

**Newcastle** a city in England known for its coal production.

**pod** here, a group of whales, usually about eight to a pod according to Ishmael.

**jaundice** an infirmity in which the eyeballs, skin, and urine become abnormally yellowish as a result of increased bile in the blood.

**paregoric** a medication that soothes or lessens pain.

**Canst thou fill . . . shaking of a spear."** Old Testament, Job 41:7, 26–34.

**effected** brought about by a cause or agent.

## Chapters 82–86
# The Honor and Glory of Whaling; Jonah Historically Regarded; Pitchpoling; The Fountain; The Tail

## Summary

Ishmael discusses the honorable profession of whaling and certain aspects of cetology. He is pleased, if a bit humbled, to belong to the "emblazoned" fraternity of whalers, whose honor is supported by history and legend. Ishmael defends the historical possibility of Jonah's story, discusses an aspect of the whale hunt, and considers two important parts of the whale.

## Commentary

Once more, Ishmael interrupts his narrative to discuss aspects of whaling and cetology that he feels are important to an understanding of the quest of the *Pequod*. Modern readers might initially disagree. For Ishmael, however, there is a significant pride in being a whaling seaman. He wants his readers to be aware that great men such as Hercules, Jonah, and even the Hindu god Vishnu are associated with whales; in addition, he is fairly certain that St. George himself actually fought a whale rather than a dragon. Those who discount the Jonah story because of the difficulty of Jonah's even passing, in one piece, to the belly of the whale, let alone surviving there, miss the point, according to Ishmael. Jonah could have been stashed away in some part of the whale's *mouth*! The reader should notice a tone of levity in all this. Melville is having a good time with his preposterous approach.

Pitchpoling is a serious matter, especially for a wounded whale. If the harpooned whale does not "sound" (dive), but runs along the surface of the sea, a hunter can inflict considerable damage with a pitchpole. This is a steel and wood (pine) spear about twelve feet in length, longer and lighter than a harpoon, easier to maneuver, and connected to a long, light rope called a "warp," which can be hauled back quickly after each darting. The hunter strikes the spear into the whale, again and again, each wound further weakening the leviathan until it dies.

The spout and the tail especially interest Ishmael, who sees mystery and grandeur in them. The spout, which looks like a fountain, is a puzzle because Ishmael can't figure out exactly how it works. It seems to have to do with breathing, because there are no gills or nose, he says, and the whale's mouth is several feet under the surface. The tail provides five functions: It is a fin for progressing; a mace in battle; a center for the sense of touch; a playful percussion instrument as it powerfully slaps the water; and a practical tool to help the whale in diving. Ishmael concludes that there is much in nature that must remain a mystery but many aspects that can be studied to reveal function.

## Glossary

**whist** a card game, a forerunner of bridge.

**mosque** a Muslim temple or place of worship.

**inveterate** settled in a habit or practice, habitual.

**vermicelli** pasta similar to spaghetti but in thinner strings.

**warp and woof** in weaving, the threads running lengthwise and crossways on the loom; the foundation upon which something is built.

**mace** a heavy medieval war club.

## Chapters 87–90
# The Grand Armada;
# Schools and Schoolmasters;
# Fast-Fish and Loose-Fish;
# Heads or Tails

## Summary

As the *Pequod* leaves the Indian Ocean and enters the straits of Sunda (dividing Sumatra and Java) bound for the China Sea, Ishmael discusses the habits of whales that move in schools and how they are governed. He then considers some of the laws of property that apply to the whaling industry, as well as an unusual right of possession in England.

## Commentary

Because whales often travel in a school, or "Grand Armada," in this part of the world, Ishmael takes the opportunity to digress regarding the structure of the schools. There are two classifications. One consists of female whales that are, when fully grown, about a third the size of an average male. A powerful bull whale, the "schoolmaster," rules these "harem schools"; his role is to breed and protect the females and to chase off any young bulls hoping to replace him. The schoolmaster reigns until he is too old to defend his harem. He then is cast out to finish his days in solitude. The other type of school consists of young bulls not yet possessing a harem. While these are not yet full-grown, they are considerably more aggressive and dangerous than the females. As they reach about three-fourths of mature size, they leave the herd and seek their own harems. Ishmael sees one other important difference in the schools. If a female is wounded, the others in the harem gather round, apparently displaying concern but sometimes endangering themselves to the same fate. When a young bull is wounded, the other males promptly desert him. Ishmael thinks he sees, in this, a gender trend consistent with humans.

The *Pequod* captures only one or two whales in the armada, but Ishmael describes the adventure in detail, including a wondrous scene (near the end of Chapter 87) taking place beneath the transparent waters. A number of mothers are nursing their young directly below the hunters. Floating on their sides, some of the mothers and their young seem to be looking right at the men above. Queequeg, looking down, confuses an umbilical cord with a harpoon line, a graphic image contrasting the beauty of nature with the harsh realities of the hunt.

The hunt reminds Ishmael that he needs to discuss property rights in whaling. They are fairly simple. A *fast-fish*, one that is lashed to a ship or in the physical possession of a crew in an open boat, belongs to those to whom it is attached. A *loose fish*, even though it may carry someone's harpoon, is fair game for anyone who can catch it. This leads Ishmael to a discussion of an oddity regarding property rights. Whales taken along the coast of England do not belong to the sailors. The whales are divided thus: the head to the king; the tail to the queen. Because whales are little more than heads or tails, the whaler is left with nothing.

## Glossary

**archipelagoes** groups or chains of many islands.

**obsequious** showing too great a willingness to serve or obey, fawning.

**concubines** here, females in the harem.

**omnivorous** eating any sort of food, eating both animal and vegetable food.

**De balena vero . . . regina caudam** Latin, "Concerning the whale, it truly suffices, if the king has the head, and the queen the tail."

**rapacious** greedy; taking by force, plundering.

## Chapters 91–92

# The *Pequod* Meets the *Rose-Bud*; Ambergris

## Summary

A week or two after the encounter with the armada, the *Pequod* comes upon an especially foul-smelling French ship called the *Bouton-de-Rose* (French, "Rose-Bud"). The source of the odor is two whales, now lashed to the ship, members of the armada and mortally wounded in the previous encounter with the men of the *Pequod*. They obviously have been dead a while. Stubb goes aboard and speaks to the French captain through an interpreter. As the *Rose-Bud* sails away, Stubb tows the smaller whale a short distance with his open boat and finds in it a valuable substance. Ahab has little interest in any of this because the *Rose-Bud* has not seen Moby Dick.

## Commentary

**Literary Device**

Melville employs the literary device of irony while describing the gam with the fragrantly titled *Bouton-de Rose*. There is irony in the name of the ship, the biography of the captain, Stubb's exchange with the captain, and the nature of (versus the source of) ambergris. In each case, the circumstance reveals a surprise, often the opposite of what might be expected.

First, the ship is French, and its name evokes not only a certain continental air of romance but also, literally, a beautiful flower with an attractive fragrance. What the crew of the *Pequod* finds is a ship with two decaying whales attached, the foul odor so strong that the *Rose-Bud* is smelled even before it is seen. The captain is a novice seaman, on his first voyage, having worked as a cologne manufacturer previously. He should have cut these whales loose long ago—or never taken them.

Stubb can't resist having some fun with the situation. Speaking to the captain through the one Englishman aboard, Stubb mocks the senior officer mercilessly. For example, he considers the captain "no more fit to command a whale-ship than a . . . monkey" and points out that he, Stubb, has "diddled" the man. The interpreter simply tells the captain that Stubb offers worthwhile advice: Cut loose the whales.

The source of ambergris is ironic. It is a valuable substance, yellow or ash in color, "unctuous and savory," used in perfume, scented candles, cooking, and as a flavor in certain wines (claret, for example). But it is found in the "inglorious bowels of a sick whale." Stubb has been at sea long enough to suspect that the offensive dead whale will contain a nice supply of the sweet, precious ambergris. He opens the whale and grabs six handfuls before Ahab insists that Stubb come back aboard ship so the *Pequod* can resume its journey.

## Glossary

**anathema** a thing or person damned or greatly detested.

**diddled** to have sexual intercourse with; here, victimized, messed with.

**slander** a false, damaging statement about a person made to another person.

**aspersion** a damaging or disparaging remark.

# Chapter 93
# The Castaway

## Summary

During the ambergris matter, Stubb's after-oarsman seriously sprained his hand, causing the second mate to assign little Pip to his boat. On his second outing, Pip leaps from the boat after it is struck by a whale and becomes tangled in the line so that Tashtego has to cut the rope, freeing Pip and saving his life but also liberating the whale. Stubb warns Pip *never* to do that again, or he will be abandoned at sea. Soon thereafter, Pip jumps again and is left alone on the ocean for a considerable time. When the *Pequod* finally picks him up, Pip has drastically changed.

## Commentary

Theme

Ishmael uses the story of Pip to demonstrate that there are depths of understanding that go beyond the limits of most mortals and that our knowledge of them may make us seem mad. Pip is a free African American, a native, we're told, of Tolland County in Connecticut. (When Ishmael calls Pip an "Alabama boy" near the end of Chapter 27, perhaps he refers to Pip's race or former family home.) Pip is a bright, sensitive, kind young fellow, not yet a man but placed among men for a difficult journey. He is, by nature, happy and peaceful. Ishmael wonders how Pip ever became "entrapped" in such a harsh business as whaling. The job does seem to have blurred his brightness, we are told.

These insights into Pip's character help to explain his problems in the boat. Pip is too young and inexperienced to be an oarsman. The first time that a whale hits the bottom of his boat, Pip, startled and afraid, leaps away—and into the line as well as the ocean. The boat loses its whale. Stubb, who is never especially sensitive, tells the child that a whale would sell for thirty times what Pip would in a slave state such as Alabama. Pip is never to be such a cowardly fool again, or he will be left at sea.

Character Insight

Soon, however, Pip jumps again, under similar circumstances. Stubb may not have meant what he said about abandoning Pip. Perhaps he was exaggerating. Maybe he thinks that the trailing boats will pick up the child, but other whales distract *them*. Whatever the reasons, Pip is left alone on the vast ocean until the mother ship fortunately finds him. He is inexorably changed. Most critics simply state that Pip becomes an "idiot," but that is not what Ishmael says. In the vast, terrible isolation of the sea, Pip has seen "God's foot upon the treadle of the loom, and spoke it; and therefore his shipmates called him mad." Pip has witnessed a cruel indifference in the universe that makes man's rational thoughts seem absurd. It is little wonder that he will become Ahab's closest—and only—friend.

## Glossary

**timorous** full of or subject to fear, timid.

**poltroon** a thorough coward.

**inexorable** that cannot be altered.

## Chapters 94–98

# A Squeeze of the Hand; The Cassock; The Try-Works; The Lamp; Stowing Down and Clearing Up

## Summary

These five chapters discuss activities aboard ship after the removal of blubber from a whale. The men work together to take the oil from the blubber, by manual labor and heat, in the bright light produced by the very oil they harvest. After the oil is cooled and sealed in casks, the crew cleans up the ship and themselves. Then the cycle begins again with another whale sighting.

## Commentary

In contrast to Pip's isolation, here (in processing the whale blubber) the men join in a communal effort that is sociable *and* businesslike. Ishmael finds it a pleasant task to squeeze the crystallized sperm oil. Sometimes his hands meet the hands of his fellows with an "abounding, affectionate, friendly, loving feeling." The camaraderie is palpable; he is overcome with serenity.

The process is imbued with certain rituals. One of the more interesting involves a mixture of fertility rite and religion. The penis of a bull whale, more than six feet in length and a foot in diameter, is cut off, lugged aboard ship, and skinned. The skin is dried, trimmed, and shaped into a rude cassock (a vestment worn by a clergyman) for the mincer, who wears it as he minces large chunks of blubber for the pots. Ishmael compares this to a religious service, the mincer a candidate for an "archbishoprick," the pun clearly intended. This ceremony is similar to some of the harvest rituals or fertility rites of agrarian societies, the whale's reproduction being essential to a continuation of the profession and symbolically honored.

## Chapters 99–100

# The Doubloon; Leg and Arm

## Summary

During one of his regular walks on the quarter-deck, Ahab fastens his attention on the gold coin that he has nailed to the mainmast, a reward for the crewman who first spots Moby Dick. Several others contemplate the coin as well. As the journey continues, Ahab hails an English ship, the *Samuel Enderby*, with his usual greeting: "Hast seen the White Whale?" This ship has. In fact, its captain lost an arm in an encounter with Moby Dick.

## Commentary

The focus returns to Ahab's egocentrism and his obsession with hunting the White Whale. As he and several other characters observe the "doubloon," the coin nailed to the mainmast and promised to the man who first sights Moby Dick, each reflects on the meaning of the coin's decorations in a way that reveals his own character. Only Ahab sees *himself* in the coin.

The shining gold doubloon has the words "REPUBLICA DEL ECUADOR: QUITO" inscribed around its border. On the face are three Andes Mountain peaks. From one comes a flame; another features a tower; on the third is a crowing cock. A portion of the zodiac arches over the coin, complete with appropriate occult signs. The sun appears at Libra. Melville suspends Ishmael's third-person narration as we move within the thoughts of each of the coin's observers.

**Character Insight**

The coin is like a mirror of the soul. Ahab sees himself in the "three peaks as proud as Lucifer" on the coin's face. For him, the tower is Ahab: firm and resolute. The volcano is Ahab: seething, powerful. The rooster is Ahab: courageous, undaunted, victorious. He thinks that the coin is "like a magician's glass, to each and every man in turn [it] but mirrors back his own mysterious self."

Others see things they value as they peruse the coin, but they don't see themselves. The devout first mate, Starbuck, sees the Trinity. Stubb sees temporary wealth and mystery. Flask reveals his inability with simple math as he miscalculates how many of his beloved cigars he could buy with the doubloon. The coin reminds Queequeg of his tattoos and homeland. The "ghost-devil" Fedallah bows to the sun that he worships. Little Pip speaks in metaphors but seems to notice a universal human longing in the coin's images. For this moment, the doubloon is the center of the ship, its "navel."

The significance of the gam with the *Samuel Enderby* is that it contrasts the two ships' captains' attitudes regarding Moby Dick. The English captain lost an arm in an encounter with the White Whale near the "Line" (equator). Unlike Ahab, however, he wants no more of the leviathan. It is best to leave the White Whale alone. Ahab does not necessarily disagree but does add, "What is best let alone, that accursed thing is not always what least allures. He's all a magnet!" The *Pequod* soon is off to continue its captain's monomaniacal quest.

# Glossary

**verdigris** a green or greenish-blue coating that forms like rust on brass, bronze, or copper.

**pilfer** to steal small sums or petty objects.

**Quito** the capital city of the republic of Ecuador.

**hoe-cake** a thin bread made of cornmeal, originally baked on a hoe at the fire.

**festoon** a wreath or garland of flowers, leaves or paper, shaped in a loop or curve.

## Chapters 101–105

# The Decanter; A Bower in the Arsacides; Measurement of the Whale's Skeleton; The Fossil Whale; Does the Whale's Magnitude Diminish?—Will He Perish?

## Summary

Because of the name of the English ship, Ishmael is set to thinking of the history of whaling, its future, and various physical aspects of the sperm whale. He himself has dissected a baby sperm and once studied the skeleton of a mature whale when he visited one of the Arsacides islands in the southwestern Pacific.

## Commentary

The history of whaling is always important to Ishmael, as is cetology. Again, he wants his audience to take these topics seriously and to place the story of the *Pequod* in their context. The English ship, which is just fading from sight, reminds him of its namesake, Samuel Enderby, a London merchant whose whaling house, in 1775, fitted out the first English ships that regularly hunted the sperm whale. Americans, notably from Nantucket, had been active in the business since 1726. Years after the gam just discussed, Ishmael visits the *Samuel Enderby*, enjoying plentiful food and drink—another indication that Ishmael will survive this story.

The narrator wants us to understand the enormity of the whale hunt and the leviathan itself. He transcribes an impressive list of supplies for whaling ships. In his own experience, he has dissected a baby sperm whale and closely studied a whale skeleton used as a shrine by aborigines in the Arsacides. Ishmael even had the measurements of that skeleton tattooed on his arm lest he forget! While he respects many aspects of cetology, he is skeptical about reports of whales that supposedly reached more than 700 feet in length. He thinks the world's largest whales live in his time, are about ninety feet long, and weigh more than ninety tons. Ishmael doubts that whales will ever become extinct, although he realizes that the buffalo have in some parts of North America. Whales, he says, have the advantage of living in vast oceans; man will never be able to hunt most of them down. As we now realize, Ishmael fails to anticipate the advance of technology, which has put sperm and other whales very much at risk in modern times.

# Glossary

**decanter** a decorative glass bottle, generally with a stopper, for serving wine.

**omniscient** knowing all things.

**The Arsacides** Pacific atolls near the southern tip of the Solomon Islands.

**fallacious** erroneous, misleading, containing a fallacy (a mistaken idea, an error in reasoning, etc.).

## Chapters 106–108
# Ahab's Leg; The Carpenter; Ahab and the Carpenter

## Summary

Entering his boat after the gam on the *Samuel Enderby*, Ahab splintered his artificial leg and needs to summon the carpenter aboard the *Pequod* to make him a new one. The carpenter is a man of many skills but little personality. Ahab is frustrated by his physical dependence on others, especially this carpenter.

## Commentary

Through the splintering of Ahab's artificial leg, Ishmael allows us to see more of the captain's character. The captain of the *Samuel Enderby* had lowered a hook to help the one-legged Ahab come aboard. When leaving the English ship, Ahab descended too quickly and broke his artificial leg as he hit his open boat. Problems with the leg annoy Ahab. He wants to feel completely independent and mentions ways in which he is—financially, for example—but his physical self carries limitations that he cannot overcome. He feels frustrated and angry.

Chapter 108 is another of the miniature dramas in the novel, complete with setting, stage directions, dialogue, and asides. The characters involved are the carpenter and Ahab. The carpenter on ship has many duties. He is a general handyman whose skills are not limited to working with wood. This one is very capable and even serves as an emergency doctor or dentist, but he seems to have no personality. His scene with Ahab is amusing because the captain soars on flights of philosophical abandon while the carpenter is stolid and mundane, his pedestrian thoughts punctuated by sporadic sneezing, which is brought on by dust from the whale bone that he shapes. Ahab finds him, and much of life, annoying: "Oh, Life! Here I am, proud as [a] Greek god, and yet standing debtor to this block-head for a bone to stand on! Cursed be that mortal inter-indebtedness."

# Glossary

**primogeniture** the exclusive right of the eldest son to inherit his father's estate.

**synod** an ecclesiastical council, a high governing body.

**stolid** having or showing little emotion or sensitivity.

**athwart** at right angles to the keel of; crosswise.

## Chapter 109
# Ahab and Starbuck in the Cabin

## Summary

The next morning, Starbuck discovers that some of the casks in the hold of the ship must be leaking oil. He finds Ahab in his cabin, poring over an ocean chart and not at all interested in being disturbed. Starbuck suggests that the ship must stop to check the casks and make whatever repairs are necessary. Ahab insists that the *Pequod*'s mission is to pursue Moby Dick and runs Starbuck off by threatening him with a musket. Shortly thereafter, Ahab relents and orders that the ship stop for inspection and repairs.

## Commentary

The problem in storage of the casks allows further insight into the characters of Starbuck and Ahab by bringing the two into direct confrontation. Twice a week, a whaler like the *Pequod*, if it is carrying any significant amount of oil, floods the hold (at the bottom of the ship) with salt water in order to keep the casks "damply tight." If oil is discovered in the water, the mariners know that some casks are leaking. When Starbuck learns of leaks in the ship's cargo, he properly reports the problem to his captain and requests permission to stop the ship and direct all hands toward investigation and repairs.

**Character Insight**

The problem reveals a stark contrast between the first mate's and the captain's conceptions of the purpose of the journey. Starbuck wants to fill the hold with oil, protect it, and return home. As he says, "What we come twenty thousand miles to get is worth saving, sir." Ahab responds, "So it is, so it is; if we get it." Starbuck means the oil; Ahab means the White Whale. Starbuck reminds the captain of the owners' interests. Ahab could not care less about the owners. He points a loaded musket toward the first mate and declares, "There is one God that is Lord over the earth, and one Captain that is lord over the *Pequod*." Ahab orders Starbuck back on deck. The first mate leaves, saying, "[L]et Ahab beware of Ahab; beware of thyself, old man." Ahab thinks about that and agrees. For whatever reason, he soon goes on deck and commands that the ship must stop for repairs. Ishmael speculates that the captain's action may be a prudent response to Starbuck's dissatisfaction.

Ahab seems relieved when Starbuck obeys his order to return to deck. Obsessed though he is, the captain realizes that he could be accused of *usurpation*, unlawfully using the ship for his own purposes rather than following the owners' directions. Starbuck, on the other hand, has only two choices. He can go along with the captain's orders or attempt to take over the ship—a drastic and extremely dangerous option even if he could convince the crew to support him. Justification for mutiny would be hard to prove, and the penalties, if he were found guilty, would be severe. Ahab's decision to repair the casks wisely resolves the situation for the time being.

## Glossary

**prating** talking much and foolishly.

**transient** temporary, passing quickly or soon.

## Chapter 110

# Queequeg in His Coffin

## Summary

Queequeg catches a chill and then a fever, "crawling about amid that dampness and slime" as he helps remove the casks from the hold. He loses weight and seems near death. Having seen canoe coffins in Nantucket that reminded him of those used on his native isle, the harpooner asks the ship's carpenter to shape him one. Trying the coffin for size, he is pleased with it but suddenly recalls some unnamed duty left undone ashore and decides to recover. Queequeg uses the coffin for a sea chest.

## Commentary

The story returns to the theme of death as one of the strongest of the crew becomes severely ill. As a harpooner, Queequeg is assigned responsibilities in the hold. The leaking casks are near the bottom of the lot, and he takes a fever during the search. The canoes that he saw in Nantucket, used for sailors' coffins, reminded the harpooner of a ritual among his aboriginal people. At his island home, the deceased are embalmed and placed in canoes but then set adrift to float away on the ocean and thence to the stars, the natives believing that each star is an island and the sky a continuation of the sea. Queequeg's sudden recovery seems amazing to most of the crew but not to him. For the aborigine, mere illness cannot kill a man unless he is willing to die; only a violent source such as a hurricane or a whale can destroy him.

Pip's visit to the apparently dying Queequeg touchingly illustrates the beauty of the little fellow's "madness" as he speaks of life and death as a journey and of himself and Queequeg as wanderers, perhaps lost souls. Pip asks Queequeg, "Poor rover! will ye never have done with all this weary roving? where go ye now?" The child requests a favor as he speaks of his former self in the third person: If Queequeg should pass the Antilles and find one Pip, missing long now, could he comfort him? Pip must be sad, says Pip, because he left his tambourine behind. Still, Pip was a coward and jumped from a whaleboat; he drowned long ago:

"Rig-a-dig, dig, dig! . . . little Pip, he died a coward; died all a'shiver;—out upon Pip!"

**Style & Language**

Melville again has used contrast for character insight. Queequeg is very matter-of-fact, almost even comic, about death. Pip is poetic and moving, the unorthodox sentence structure of the passage indicating the child's state of mind.

## Glossary

**tierce**  a forty-two gallon cask.

**sinecure**  here, an office or position requiring little work.

**nigh**  near in time or place.

**apprised**  informed.

**Antilles**  the main island group of the West Indies, including all but the Bahamas.

**hieroglyphic**  a picture or sign representing a word; difficult to understand.

## Chapters 111–114
# The Pacific;
# The Blacksmith;
# The Forge;
# The Gilder

## Summary

As the *Pequod* enters the "sweet mystery" of the Pacific Ocean, Ishmael understands why most seamen find serenity in these vast waters. That is not the case with Ahab. His purpose intensifies as he prepares for the meeting with the White Whale. The captain asks his blacksmith, Perth, to shape him an especially powerful harpoon. We learn the tragic history of Perth's background and witness a demonic baptism of Ahab's new weapon.

## Commentary

These short chapters begin the final movement of the novel toward a showdown between Ahab and Moby Dick. The serenity of the Pacific contrasts with the turbulence in the captain's soul as he senses that the White Whale must be very near.

Style & Language

Only rarely does Melville stereotype, but Perth's story is told with the excessive sentimentality and predictability of melodrama. Ahab feels compassion for Perth, the ship's blacksmith. In him he sees a fellow wounded human being. At the age of sixty, Perth had been a successful artisan with a youthful, "daughter-like" wife, a comfortable home, and three happy, healthy children. We learn that Perth's life was ruined by alcohol, the "Bottle Conjuror" letting loose an evil spirit: "Upon the opening of that fatal cork, forth flew the fiend, and shriveled up his [Perth's] home." Perth failed at his work. His wife died or, as Ishmael puts it, "dived down into the long church-yard grass." Two children followed her. Perth lost everything, including toes to frostbite one bitter wintry night, resulting in a "yawing in his gait." When Ahab asks Perth why the sparks of the forge don't burn him, the blacksmith responds, "I am past scorching; not easily can'st thou scorch a scar."

Ahab's dark motives become more clear as he has Perth shape a powerful harpoon out of strong steel nails from racing horses' shoes. The captain asks the three pagan harpooners on board to provide the point with a "true death-temper" of their own blood, which they do. In a baptism ritual that would please Satan, Ahab covers the barb with that blood and speaks a Latin alteration of the Christian sacrament: "*Ego non baptizo te in nomine patris, sed in nomine diaboli!*" ("I do not baptize thee in the name of the father, but in the name of the devil.")

## Glossary

**supplication**  a humble request or prayer.

**blithe**  cheerful, carefree.

**conjurer**  a magician, sorcerer.

**oblivious**  unaware, unmindful, forgetful.

**abated**  made less in amount, degree, or force.

## Chapter 115

# The *Pequod* Meets the *Bachelor*

## Summary

A few weeks after the welding of Ahab's harpoon, the *Pequod* meets a Nantucket ship called the *Bachelor*, a whaler filled with oil and headed home. The crew of the *Bachelor* "vaingloriously" celebrates its success, and the two captains briefly share their very different opinions.

## Commentary

Literary
Device

The episode with the *Bachelor* is one of the novel's most effective examples of the use of contrast and detail. The *Bachelor* contrasts with the *Virgin* (Chapter 81) in that its crew and captain are experienced, skilled whalers who are at the end of a successful voyage. In addition to their abilities, they have been blessed with good luck and have filled the ship with oil while other vessels in the same seas, reminiscent of the *Virgin* when it was met, have sometimes gone for months without capturing a single whale. The *Bachelor*'s hold is bursting with casks of sperm oil. Barrels of food, no longer needed on the shortened journey, have been given away to make more room—or traded for supplemental casks. Barrels of oil are stowed on deck and in the officers' and even the captain's quarters, the officers' mess table removed and burned to make more room. Crewmen have caulked and pitched their sea chests, turning them into makeshift casks for more and more oil. Someone jokes that the cook has filled his largest boiler with oil and the steward his spare coffeepot. Everything is filled with oil, Ishmael says, except the captain's trouser pockets.

Even more significant is the contrast with the *Pequod*. The *Bachelor* is a happy ship devoted only to its professional mission of accumulating oil and returning safely home to Nantucket. The mood aboard ship is light and bursting with revelry as opposed to the *Pequod*'s ominous anticipation of its dark goal, pursuing Moby Dick. The *Bachelor* sails with the wind to its back; the *Pequod* fights the wind. Even from a distance, it is easy to mark the celebration aboard the *Bachelor* as it proudly and joyfully displays ensigns and jacks of all colors. The men at the mastheads wear streamers of red bunting. Containers of oil are lashed to the masts and to the lookout posts as trophies, no more sightings of whales necessary. The lower jaw of the last whale taken hangs from a spar at the front of the ship; at the rear, an open boat hangs upside down. Drums sound from the forecastle. There is music and dancing with "olive-hued girls who had eloped" from the Polynesian Isles. The try-works have been torn down, no further rendering of blubber needed.

**Character Insight**

Most striking are the contrasting demeanors of the two captains. The *Bachelor*'s commander is jovial and hospitable, inviting Ahab to come aboard for a drink. Ahab grits his teeth, ignores the invitation, and asks, of course, "Hast seen the White Whale?" The other captain says he has only heard of the leviathan but doesn't believe in him. Ahab is obsessed with killing that which the practical, successful captain deems a myth. Ahab decides that the other man is "too damned jolly . . . How wondrous familiar [chummy] is a fool!" he mutters. The *Bachelor*'s pilot announces that it is "a full ship and homeward-bound." Ahab's revealing reply sums up the contrast: "Thou art a full ship and homeward bound, thou sayst; well, then, call me an empty ship, and outward-bound."

## Glossary

**vainglorious** boastfully vain and proud of oneself.

**bowsprit** a large, tapered spar extending forward from the bow of a sailing vessel.

**jacks** here, small flags.

**taffrail** the rail around the stern of a ship.

## Chapters 116–119

# The Dying Whale;
# The Whale Watch;
# The Quadrant;
# The Candles

## Summary

Some of the *Bachelor*'s good fortune seems to have transferred to the *Pequod*, which captures four whales in one day. Ahab's boat stays out to guard one whale overnight, during which time Fedallah offers the captain an important prophecy. As the *Pequod* heads for the equator and the anticipated meeting with Moby Dick, Ahab destroys his quadrant, complaining that it only tells him where he *is*, not where he *shall* be or, more important, where Moby Dick is. The ship encounters a typhoon, which Ahab refuses to allow to defeat him.

## Commentary

The dark, ominous atmosphere, almost a feeling of doom, increases aboard the *Pequod* despite the capture of four whales. Spending the night with his private crew on their open boat, guarding one of the whales that could not be taken to the ship in daylight, Ahab wakens to tell Fedallah of a recurring dream about hearses. The mysterious Fedallah then reminds Ahab of a private prophecy, which he now expands. When Ahab dies, he will have no use for either a hearse or a coffin, according to Fedallah. Before he can die on this voyage, the captain must see two hearses on the sea. One will not be made by mortal hands; the other will display wood grown in America. Fedallah will die before Ahab but later appear to the captain and serve as his guide. Finally, only a hemp rope can kill Ahab. The captain is first amused and then confused by the prophecy. How can there be hearses on the sea? And how can he die by rope—the gallows? No, Ahab must live forever if these prophecies are to come true. He will "slay Moby Dick and survive it!"

**Character Insight**

The sudden typhoon challenges even Ahab's fury and reveals more of his character. The crew wants to flee the storm, but Ahab insists on fighting it. His response to the power of nature is defiance. We learn conclusively that a lightning bolt caused Ahab's long scar, but he does not cower when lightning sets the three masts to flaming like some giant religious candelabra. When his own harpoon is set ablaze, he brandishes it at the crew, threatening to impale the first sailor to quit his post. Starbuck pleads with him: "God, God is against thee, old man; forbear! @'tis an ill voyage!" Ahab stands fast. He reminds the crew of the oaths they took to hunt the White Whale. Finally, he claims to "blow out the last fear" and, with a blast of breath, he extinguishes his harpoon's flame.

# Glossary

**weal** well-being, welfare.

**effulgent** radiant, brilliant.

**Mene, Mene, Tekel Upharsin** a cryptic biblical phrase from Daniel 5: 5, 25–28, which Daniel sees as a curse from God. Here, Melville is illustrating the gravity of the situation.

**tableau** a striking, dramatic scene or picture.

## Chapters 120–124

# The Deck towards the End of the First Night Watch; Midnight—The Forecastle Bulwarks; Midnight Aloft— Thunder and Lightning; The Musket; The Needle

## Summary

As the typhoon continues, Ahab holds his course. Representative of the crew, Stubb sees things the captain's way. A few hours after midnight, the storm abates; following orders to inform Ahab of any change, Starbuck heads for the captain's cabin where Ahab is asleep. Starbuck sees an opportunity to shoot his commander and end the madness, but he cannot. Next morning, Ahab finds the storm has passed, but the ship's compass has gone awry. He makes a new one, proudly indicating his obsessive dominance.

## Commentary

**Style & Language**

In some of these chapters, Melville returns to a dramatic format and presents scenes with stage directions, dialogue, soliloquy, and comic relief. (A short, frivolous speech by Tashtego calls for more rum and less thunder.) The scenes allow the story to progress with only significant snippets of action instead of detailing the progress of the storm and the crew's reaction throughout the night. We might think of the storm as representative of the turmoil in Ahab's soul *or* the troubled resolution of purpose as the *Pequod* goes through the final steps required to bring everyone together, working toward a single goal of hunting Moby Dick.

Ahab and Starbuck are still in conflict when the first mate pleads with Ahab, in Chapter 120, to bring down the main topsail and give in to the force of the typhoon. Ahab adamantly refuses. He seems to see himself in a mortal struggle with nature or even God and is not about to relent: "Strike nothing; lash it . . . . By masts and keels! he takes me for the hunchbacked skipper of some coasting smack." Representative of much of the crew, Stubb accedes to Ahab's will and follows the captain's orders no matter how dangerous they may seem.

When the storm lets up after midnight (Chapter 123), Ahab is asleep in his cabin. Now Starbuck must face *his* moment of truth. He is in a moral dilemma. In a soliloquy with stage directions implied by the speech, Starbuck considers using a loaded musket, which Ahab once pointed at Starbuck, to kill the captain. A touch on the musket's trigger could end the madness and allow the first mate to see his wife, Mary, and his son again. Such an act would end one life; but if he takes no action, he realizes that he and the crew may all be dead within a week. The first mate seems to be "wrestling with an angel." Ultimately, he cannot kill his captain. For good or ill, it is beyond Starbuck's moral capacity. Attempting to arrest Ahab is impractical under the circumstances. Starbuck returns to the deck without disturbing the ship's commander. Thus, even he acquiesces.

## Glossary

**helm**  the wheel by which a ship is steered.

**smack**  a small sailboat, usually rigged as a sloop with only mainsail and jib.

**lucifers**  lucifer, an early type of friction match.

**shuttlecock**  a rounded, feathered piece of cork used as the "bird" in badminton.

**crucible**  a container that can resist great heat, used for melting ore; a test or trial.

**abashed**  embarrassed, self-conscious.

## Chapters 125–127

# The Log and Line;
# The Life-Buoy;
# The Deck

## Summary

Ahab has the carpenter put together a log and line, replacing the old, rotted apparatus, in order to help him discern the ship's direction and speed. Pip comes to help his captain and so touches Ahab with his madness and sense of loss that the commander takes the child under wing. A sailor falls from the mainmast, drowning when the ship's old life buoy won't float. The carpenter makes a buoy out of Queequeg's coffin.

## Commentary

Ahab's personal control of the ship's fate is further represented by his replacement of the log and line. With this device, a log is attached to the rear of the ship by a long line so that the captain can have some further idea of how the craft is steering and of its speed. Ahab welcomes the opportunity to take charge completely: "I crush the quadrant, the thunder turns the needles, and now the mad sea parts the log-line. But Ahab can mend all."

**Character Insight**

The captain's compassionate side is touched by little Pip, who comes to help. As he did with the blacksmith, Ahab identifies with this wounded, lost soul. He also sees in Pip further evidence of a cold and cruel universal power: "There can be no hearts above the snow-line. Oh, ye frozen heavens! look down here. Ye did beget this luckless child, and have abandoned him, ye creative libertines." Ahab joins hands with Pip and vows to keep him close.

Turning Queequeg's canoe-coffin-sea chest into a life buoy foreshadows the ending of the novel and renews the theme of death, now contrasted with life and rebirth. Ahab, always struggling with these enormous topics, considers the symbolism: "Can it be that in some spiritual sense the coffin is, after all, but an immortality preserver!" The coffin will play a practical role in helping Ishmael live to tell his tale.

## Glossary

**oblique** having a slanted position or direction.

**libertines** people who live unrestrained, immoral lives.

**bodings** here, ominous, foreboding thoughts.

## Chapter 128

# The *Pequod* Meets the *Rachel*

## Summary

The next day, a large Nantucket whaler called the *Rachel* approaches the *Pequod*. Its captain is an acquaintance of Ahab. In response to Ahab's usual first question ("Hast seen the White Whale?"), the *Rachel's* captain reports that his fastest whaleboat, with his own son aboard, has just recently been lost at sea due to an encounter with Moby Dick. He entreats Ahab to help in the search. The *Pequod's* commander staunchly refuses and sets sail in pursuit of his only goal.

## Commentary

The contrast between a loving father's concern for his son and an obsessed madman's concern only for personal revenge against a whale is chilling. Moby Dick's role in the loss of Captain Gardiner's son adds to the mystery surrounding the White Whale. The *Rachel's* three regular whaleboats were four or five miles windward from the mother ship, in chase of a large group of whales. Suddenly, Moby Dick appeared downwind. The captain sent his reserve boat, with his son as part of the crew, in pursuit of the White Whale. From what the lookouts could see, the boat seemed to fasten (by harpoon) with Moby Dick, who then sped off with the boat in tow. It was unclear what happened next, but the boat may have been sunk. Or it could still be out there. Any sane whaling man would help the *Rachel* in its search. Never mind that the captains are acquaintances; or that Ahab has been offered generous remuneration; or that he, too, has a son. *Any* reasonable captain would join in this search.

Nevertheless, there is no ambiguity in Ahab's response. We can hear every distinct syllable as he responds in a voice that "prolongingly" shapes each word: "Captain Gardiner, I will not do it. Even now I lose time . . . . I must go." Without a second thought, Ahab gives the order to sail.

# Glossary

**shoal** a large group or school of fish.

**stunsail** studdingsail, an auxiliary sail designed to increase speed in light winds.

**boon** a request for a favor; the favor granted.

**Rachel, weeping for her children** a biblical reference, Jeremiah 31: 15 and Matthew 2: 18.

## Chapters 129–132

# The Cabin; The Hat;
# The *Pequod* Meets the *Delight*;
# The Symphony

## Summary

Shortly after meeting the *Rachel*, Ahab distances himself from Pip because he fears a softening of determination in the presence of the child. Growing distrustful of his crew, the captain insists on taking the mainmast watch himself in hopes of spotting the White Whale. A red-billed sea-hawk steals his hat shortly after Ahab is lifted to the lookout post. The *Pequod* has an ominous gam with the ironically named *Delight*. Ahab has an important moment of reflection as the encounter with Moby Dick grows near.

## Commentary

The tone of the novel grows even darker, increasingly ominous as the *Pequod* sails closer and closer to Moby Dick. Ahab feels himself growing too soft with Pip and finds it necessary to distance himself from the loving child. He feels that Pip is "too curing to my malady. Like cures like; and for this hunt, my malady becomes my most desired health." Ahab will allow no serenity or sanity to deter him. A creeping paranoia causes the captain to distrust his crew. Perhaps some on watch have seen the White Whale but failed to call out! Ahab himself takes the lookout at the mainmast, lifted to the post in a basket. A hawk toys with him, one more taunting gesture from nature, and steals his hat, which Ishmael sees as an evil omen.

The meeting with the *Delight* reminds us of the dangers of the impending encounter. As usual, Ahab calls out, "Hast seen the White Whale?" Indeed, the *Delight*'s captain has, as evidenced by a smashed whaleboat and a funeral even now taking place aboard ship. One seaman is being buried; the White Whale sent four others directly to their ocean graves the previous day. Ahab wants no part in this recognition of defeat. He orders the *Pequod* to sail on—but not soon enough to avoid hearing the splash of the corpse as it hits the sea.

**Character Insight**

Ahab has one last moment of reflection before the chase begins with Moby Dick. It is a gorgeous day on the Pacific as Ahab crosses the deck and gazes over the rail. Starbuck joins him. Ahab recalls his forty years at sea, harpooning his first whale at age eighteen; finally marrying—a much younger girl—when he was past fifty; sailing for Cape Horn the next day. Of those forty years, he has not spent three ashore. He calls himself a "fool." But when Starbuck attempts to persuade him to turn back and go home, Ahab says he is no longer in control of his fate: "What is it, what nameless, inscrutable, unearthly thing is it; what cozening, hidden lord and master, and cruel, remorseless emperor commands me?" This is the beginning of the greatest speech in the novel, near the end of Chapter 132, a soliloquy (only a page long) that should be read aloud and in full to be appreciated.

The captain is no stereotype and certainly is no ordinary man. He is a complicated, deep, tortured soul. He even knows he is mad, but he cannot stop himself. Ahab contemplates the beauties of life and death as he notices that "the air smells now, as if it blew from a far-away meadow; they have been making hay somewhere under the slopes of the Andes, Starbuck, and the mowers are sleeping among the new-mown hay." We all will sleep at last in one place or another. We will sleep and "rust amid greenness." Ahab is ready to die. Unfortunately, he will take his crew with him.

## Glossary

**epaulet** a shoulder ornament for uniforms, especially for military officers' uniforms.

**fain** gladly willing

**tremulous** trembling, timid, fearful.

**cozening** cheating, deceiving.

## Chapters 133–135

# The Chase—First Day; The Chase—Second Day; The Chase—Third Day

## Summary

That night, while standing at his pivot hole on deck, Ahab suddenly catches the scent of whale. At dawn, he notices an impressive, sleek wake of a large whale and soon spots Moby Dick. The chase begins. The White Whale sinks Ahab's whaleboat that first day. Moby Dick prevails the second day as well, smashing boats and apparently killing Fedallah. On the third day, Fedallah's prophecy (see Chapter 117) mysteriously proves true. The wounded whale attacks and sinks the *Pequod*. In a desperate last attempt to harpoon the leviathan from his open boat, Ahab inadvertently becomes entangled in the hemp harpoon line and is cast into the sea to his death.

## Commentary

The last three chapters of the novel contain some of the finest descriptions of dramatic action in American literature. They should be read as a unit. As the chase develops, Ahab becomes aware that Fedallah's prophecy is proving true in ways that the captain could not have anticipated.

Ahab has never doubted that his destiny is to confront the White Whale. Appropriately, he takes control of the chase from the beginning. Like a trained hound, he catches the scent of his prey during the night following his talk with Starbuck. At dawn, Ahab notices a smooth wake on the ocean, probably left by a large whale. The captain insists on taking the mainmast watch. He is not more than two-thirds of the way to the top when he shouts, "There she blows!—there she blows! A hump like a snow-hill! It is Moby Dick!" The boats are lowered, but the White Whale soon sounds (dives) and disappears for an hour. Suddenly a flock of white birds grows excited and approaches Ahab's boat, indicating that the whale they follow is near. At first the captain sees nothing. Then, peering toward the depths, he notices a small white spot emerging. It grows. Soon it is huge. It is Moby Dick. Ahab attempts evasion. It is too late. The enormous jaws of the White Whale chop his boat in two: "[A]s if perceiving this stratagem, Moby Dick, with that malicious intelligence ascribed to him, . . . in the manner of a biting shark, slowly and feelingly taking its [the boat's] bows full within his mouth, . . . shook the slight cedar as a mildly cruel cat her mouse . . . . [and] bit the craft completely in twain." Ahab is rescued, but that day's hunt is over.

Moby Dick seems too intelligent to be a mere fish. He manipulates each encounter like an experienced battle general. The second day, Ahab again spots his prey. The whaleboats' harpooners manage to hit Moby Dick with several barbs, but the wise leviathan uses this misfortune to his advantage. Turning on the boats, he draws them together by the harpoon ropes connected to the whale, smashing two of the boats "like two rolling husks on a surf-beaten beach." He then uses his head to flip Ahab's boat into the air, landing it upside down and leaving the crew to scramble out from under it "like seals from a sea-side cave." Ahab's ivory leg is broken. At first it seems that no one is killed. Later we learn that Fedallah is missing.

One of the devices that Melville sometimes uses in these chapters is to allow the characters to set the mood through their reactions. On the third day, Ahab again sights the whale. Upon contact, he sees that Fedallah has become shockingly lashed to Moby Dick's back, the prophet's eyes open and staring at the captain: "Aye, Parsee! I see thee again.—Aye, and thou goest before; and this, *this* then is the hearse that thou didst promise." All boats except Ahab's are damaged and return to the ship. Ahab manages to sink his fierce harpoon "and his fiercer curse" into the whale; but Moby Dick attacks the *Pequod* itself and smashes the starboard bow (right front) of the ship, sinking the vessel. From his open boat, Ahab reacts to the sinking of his proud vessel: "The ship! The hearse!—the second hearse! . . . Oh! ye three unsurrendered spires of mine; thou uncracked keel; . . . thou firm deck, . . . must ye then perish, and without me?" In a last, desperate effort, Ahab throws one more harpoon at Moby Dick but becomes entangled in the hemp line and is tossed to the sea and his death. The ship sinks in a vortex that takes all but one down with it.

The mystery of Fedallah's prophecy has been solved through the action of the chase. As it turned out, Ahab had neither a hearse nor a coffin. Fedallah died before the captain but was seen by Ahab again and served as his guide toward death. Ahab saw two hearses: one *not* made by mortal hands (the White Whale carrying Fedallah's corpse); the other (the *Pequod*) made of wood grown in America. Finally, a hemp rope killed Ahab, sending him directly to the depths of the sea.

Death has come to the *Pequod* and made of it a hearse. Continuing the funeral motif, Melville writes of the sea as a "great shroud" that soon rests over the dead and rolls on as it has for five thousand years, the biblical chronology of time since the Great Flood of Noah's day (Genesis 5:28–10:32).

## Glossary

**wont** usual practice, habit.

**palpable** that which can be touched, felt, or handled; tangible.

**shiver** here, to cause a sail to flutter by heading too close to the wind.

**allured** tempted with something desirable, enticed.

**prescience** apparent knowledge of things before they happen, foreknowledge.

# Epilogue

## Summary

Ishmael explains his survival. In Fedallah's absence, he had rowed with Ahab that last day. He was tossed from the boat and floated "on the margin of the ensuing scene" but within full sight of the action. By the time the vortex pulled him to its center, it had sufficiently subsided so that he was not sucked under. Suddenly Queequeg's coffin buoy shot up from the center of the fading vortex. Clinging to it for a day and a night, Ishmael finally was rescued by the *Rachel*, "that in her retracing search after her missing children, only found another orphan."

## Commentary

In the brief, poetic epilogue, Melville provides a practical solution to one of the early criticisms of the novel. The epilogue was added after the first British printing, which drew criticism because the story appeared to be told by a dead man.

The conclusion unites the themes of friendship and death, suggesting that it is Queequeg's love for his friend that saves Ishmael. Queequeg's coffin has served as a sea chest and the ship's life buoy. Now it turns from a symbol of death to a practical means of survival, even rebirth, for the narrator who is then rescued by the very ship that Ahab previously had refused to help.

## Glossary

**"And I only am escaped alone to tell thee"** a biblical reference to Job 1:17.

# CHARACTER ANALYSES

# Ahab

Long before Ahab's first appearance, there is an air of mystery about the captain of the *Pequod*. The owners hire the crew in Ahab's absence. When Ishmael inquires about the captain, he is told that Ahab is a man of few words but deep meaning; from the first, it is clear that the captain is a complicated character. He is a "grand, ungodly, god-like" man who has been in colleges as well as among the cannibals. This brief introduction reveals significant information. Ahab is ungodly in that he refuses to submit to any higher power. He does not worship or even acknowledge the superiority of forces beyond himself. Ahab is god-like in that he is larger than life. Perhaps he even wants to *be* God.

The mystery continues as Ahab remains in his cabin through the early days of the voyage. Ishmael grows increasingly uneasy, checking the area outside the captain's cabin whenever the narrator goes on watch. When Ahab finally appears on his quarter-deck (Chapter 28), he is an imposing, frightening figure whose haunted visage sends shivers over Ishmael. The captain looks like a man "cut away from the stake, when the fire has overrunningly wasted all the limbs without consuming them, or taking away one particle from their compacted aged robustness." A white scar, reportedly from a thunderbolt, runs down his face and, some say, the length of his body. Ahab does seem godlike, or at least mythic, from the beginning. He is surrounded by legend, cured by lightning, grim, determined. We learn early on that an equally legendary White Whale has bitten off one of the captain's legs. A prosthesis replaces it, fashioned from another sperm whale's jaw. The man is thus part whale himself, part lightning bolt; he feels a thunderous electricity within himself. If Ahab is mad, he is madness personified, a huge man, larger than life, legendary, god-like.

Ahab is a man of great depth but few words. When he speaks, others listen because he moves them with charismatic persuasion. In the pivotal Chapter 36, Ahab finally gathers the crewmen together and, in a rousing speech, solicits their support in a single purpose for this voyage: hunting down and killing the White Whale. He first unifies the group by asking a series of emotionally charged questions that call for collective responses: What do you do when you spot a whale? What do you do next? What tune do you pull to in pursuit? The men are increasingly excited, as if they are in the blood lust of a real hunt. Ahab then employs his prop, a Spanish gold ounce, offering it to the lookout who first sees ("raises") the White Whale. The end of Ahab's oration unites all of the crewmen except for Starbuck in the monomaniacal goal of pursuing Moby Dick.

Ahab's *quest* is grand, ungodly, and god-like. Starbuck accuses the captain of blasphemy for seeking revenge against a "dumb brute . . . that simply smote thee from blindest instinct" (Chapter 36). For Ahab, blasphemy is no vice. He would "strike the sun if it insulted me." The captain wants to take on the structure of nature, even God himself. To him, Moby Dick is not just some dumb brute. The White Whale is a façade, a mask, behind which lurks the "inscrutable thing," the force that is Ahab's true enemy. Ahab is certain that the force is evil. Others find the evil in Ahab's ego, in his own soul. To understand Ahab, we must understand that it is this force behind the mask that Ahab really wants to kill. Ahab believes that the force wants to injure him, to limit his role in the world. Perhaps he is right. Perhaps the force *is* evil. Or perhaps Ahab is madness itself, striking out against the essential powers of the universe, which he cannot possibly defeat. In either case, his quest is bold and literally magnificent. If Ahab is mad, as even he concedes that he is, it is a huge madness, containing multitudes. Part of the universal appeal of the book is that this is a madness to which many briefly aspire, from time to time, resisting our limited, petty roles in the universe. For most, it is just a fleeting yearning and clearly beyond our grasps. For Ahab, it is everything.

We see a different side of Ahab the day before the *Pequod's* first encounter with the White Whale. Starbuck and the captain are at the rail in the sunshine and soft breezes. For the most part, Ahab is a static character, one who does not grow or change throughout the novel due to his single-minded obsession. But here he briefly wavers. Ahab recalls his forty years at sea, harpooning his first whale at age eighteen; finally marrying when he was past fifty; sailing for Cape Horn the next day. Of those forty years, he has not spent three ashore. He calls himself a "fool." But when Starbuck tries to persuade him to turn back and go home, Ahab says he is no longer in control of his fate: "What is it, what nameless, inscrutable, unearthly thing is it; what cozening, hidden lord and master, and cruel, remorseless emperor commands me?" This is the beginning of the greatest speech in the novel, near the end of Chapter 132, a soliloquy that should be read aloud to fully appreciate Ahab's character. Like the figure behind the mask of the White Whale, the force behind Ahab's motivation is also an inscrutable, dominating master. In his madness, perhaps Ahab is fighting evil or nature or God; or perhaps he is simply fighting Ahab.

The captain is no stereotype and certainly is no ordinary man. He is a complicated, deep, tortured soul. Even though he knows he is mad, he cannot stop himself. Ahab contemplates the beauties as well as the horrors of life and death as he smells the sweet air blowing over the Pacific. He muses that mowers have been making hay somewhere beneath the slopes of the Andes and are "sleeping among the new-mown hay." We all sleep at last, he thinks, sleep and "rust amid greenness." Or at the depths of the ocean.

The final three days leave no time for contemplation as Ahab finally encounters Moby Dick. The captain's final defeat seems inevitable. Time and again, the White Whale out-maneuvers the crew of the *Pequod*, once even using the lines of the harpoons, which the men have lodged in the whale, to whiplash and smash their boats. Ahab's final attempt to kill his nemesis results in his own death as the hemp line of the captain's harpoon lodges around his own neck, casting him to his death in the sea.

# Ishmael

The narrator is an observant young man from Manhattan, perhaps even as young as Melville was (twenty-one) when he first sailed as a crew member on the American whaler *Acushnet*. Ishmael tells us that he often seeks a sea voyage when he gets to feeling glum. Four times he has sailed in the merchant service (so he may well be in his mid-twenties or older). This time he has a yearning for a voyage on a whaling ship. Thus we have a story—because of Ishmael's desire for a whaling venture, his keen observation, his ability to spin a yarn, his ability to grow and learn, and his unique survival. If Ishmael doesn't live, we have no story.

Ishmael probably is a more interesting narrator because he is a loner by nature. This allows him further objectivity and a freedom of evaluation that more involvement might dissuade. Melville frequently employs biblical allusions as keys to understanding in the novel, and he does so here. The biblical Ishmael (Genesis 16:1–16; 21:10 ff.) is disinherited and dismissed from his home in favor of his half-brother Isaac. The name suggests that the narrator is something of an outcast, a drifter, a fellow of no particular family other than mankind. Ishmael confirms his independent ways by telling us that he seeks no special rank aboard ship and would not want to be either a cook or a captain; he says he has enough responsibility just taking care of himself.

Ishmael speaks of no family or even a last name. This is consistent with the ending of the book in which only Ishmael survives, picked up by the whaling ship *Rachel*, which, searching after its own missing children, finds only "another orphan" (Epilogue).

Ishmael's isolation makes his one real friendship, with the Polynesian harpooner Queequeg, all the more important. Part of Ishmael's appeal as a narrator is that he is an open-minded character who is capable of change and growth. When he first meets Queequeg, in a bed they share at the Spouter-Inn, Ishmael is terrified. He sees the South Seas islander as a stereotypical "heathen" and fears that he is about to be killed by a cannibal. Just the opposite is true. Ishmael soon learns that Queequeg is one of the finest men he has ever known—caring, kind, generous, loyal, courageous, and wise. Together, they explore the rich possibilities existing in diversity. Ultimately, it is this acceptance that indirectly saves Ishmael's life.

# Moby Dick

The novel is named after Moby Dick because he is the center of Ahab's obsession and a key figure in his own right. The White Whale's appearance is unique. He is an exceptionally large sperm whale with a snow-white head, wrinkled brow, crooked jaw, and an especially bushy spout. His hump is also white and shaped like a pyramid; the rest of his body is marbled with white. He has three holes in the right fluke of his tail, and he fantails oddly before he submerges.

The White Whale seems to have an almost human personality, featuring the battle savvy of a bold general. One of his favorite tricks is to seem to be fleeing from hunters but suddenly turn to attack and destroy their open boats. When engaged with the crew of the *Pequod*, he sounds (dives) and then reappears in their midst before they can escape or counter his attack. When they lodge harpoons in him, he uses the attaching ropes to whiplash and destroy their boats. In a final show of timely brute force, he crashes into the bow of the *Pequod* itself and quickly sinks her.

These are the facts. Equally important are the legends and suspicions regarding Moby Dick. He is said to be immortal and omnipresent, supposedly appearing in several locations at the same time. Most significant is what he means to Ahab. The captain sees the White Whale as a great mask, a façade behind which is some "inscrutable thing," an undefined power that Ahab resents and seeks to destroy. Each reader must confront this problem: Is Moby Dick a mask for some great force of evil? Is he a figure of nature that hides, perhaps, the face of God? Or is he just a big, clever fish that would leave men alone if they would stop bothering him?

# Queequeg

The amiable Polynesian harpooner contributes significantly to the themes of friendship and diversity in the novel. Although Queequeg is a heathen, by Christian definition, Ishmael increasingly notices the man's independent dignity, good heart, extraordinary courage, and generous spirit. Queequeg's body is covered with tattoos, and Ishmael initially assumes that the aborigine must be a cannibal. He soon learns that his new friend is one of the most civilized men that he has ever met. As Ishmael concludes, "You cannot hide the soul" (Chapter 10).

Born a prince, Queequeg gave up a life of ease on his native island, Kokovoko, when he stole aboard a visiting whaling ship and insisted on joining the crew. His purpose was to experience the world of which he had only heard stories. Ishmael, too, wants to see the world. What they discover is that a man's soul is more important than his appearance or even his religion.

Ishmael has sensed his friend's noble spirit. In fact, almost immediately Ishmael recognizes Queequeg's noble character, noting that he "treated me with so much civility and consideration, while I was guilty of great rudeness." Queequeg is a synthesis of all racial and ethnic characteristics; that is, he is a symbol of all mankind. His signature is the symbol for infinity.

Although the theme of friendship receives less consideration once the *Pequod* sails, Queequeg indirectly saves Ishmael's life. Twice, the harpooner rescues men from drowning—a bumpkin who has been mocking him and Tashtego, another harpooner. While working in the hold of the ship, Queequeg takes a fever. Near death, he has the ship's carpenter fashion him a coffin in the shape of a canoe, reminiscent of those on his home island. Just as everyone has given up hope, Queequeg remembers some duties left undone and decides to live a while after all. The coffin becomes his sea chest and later, caulked and pitched, the ship's life buoy. At the end of the novel, when Moby Dick sinks the *Pequod*, the life-buoy coffin suddenly pops to the surface, allowing Ishmael to cling to it and survive until the *Rachel* rescues him.

## Starbuck

The first mate is the only man aboard the *Pequod* who resists Ahab's plan to devote the ship's mission to hunting and killing the White Whale. Starbuck contrasts with Ahab in his spirit and manner. Where Ahab is bombastic, outrageous, and monomaniac, Starbuck is prudent, calm, and reasonable. But he lacks Ahab's power. The chief mate argues that the ship's mission, as prescribed by the owners, is to harvest as much whale oil as possible and return home safely, showing a profit. He feels it is "blasphemous" to be enraged by a dumb object of nature such as a whale, and he realizes that the lives of all aboard are at serious risk. At one point (Chapter 123), Starbuck even considers shooting the captain to end the madness. Ultimately, however, Starbuck acquiesces. He concedes that he is no match for the enormity of the charismatic captain's spirit. Even though he is certain that Ahab is mad, Starbuck cannot take the action necessary to stop him. Perhaps he is too moral to kill or feels bound to a higher duty. At any rate, the first mate obeys orders. As a character, he changes only because he submits to Ahab.

## Fedallah

The leader of the "five dusky phantoms," whom Ahab has secretly brought aboard to serve as his private boat crew, is the mysterious Fedallah, who serves as the captain's harpooner. An ancient Asian, he is reported to be a Parsee—a member of a religious sect descended from the Persians and devoted to the teachings of the prophet Zoroaster in the sixth century B.C., contrasting the spirits of light or good (*Ormazd*) with the spirits of darkness or evil (*Ahriman*). Here, the significance is that Fedallah is a man of mystery, a non-Christian who seems to be Ahab's guide or guru. Some critics suggest that, because Fedallah is a Parsee and supposedly devoted to good, he is a double agent, an assassin sent by God to eliminate Ahab. (If one considers that the Parsees were "devoted to "doing God's work" as opposed to "devoted to good," it is possible that Fedallah is doing both. Given Ahab's perspective of God and the universe, this interpretation of Fedallah and his role is valid.)

Through his actions, though, Ahab's guide seems more demonic—perhaps a Parsee who shares Ahab's madness and perceives the same evil that the captain sees. In either case, Fedallah contributes to the rich ambiguity surrounding Ahab. The Parsee's prophecy regarding the captain comes true in surprising ways near the end of the novel.

# Father Mapple

A venerable, vigorous man of God, Father Mapple sets the tone for the novel in his sermon at the Whaleman's Chapel (Chapter 9). A harpooner in his youth, the parson frequently alludes to the imagery of seamen in his sermon, referring to the congregation, for example, as his "shipmates." Ascending to his pulpit by climbing a rope ladder like one used to mount a ship from a boat at sea, Mapple appropriately employs, as his text, the Old Testament story of Jonah and the whale. Ahab could benefit from Mapple's theme: "And if we obey God, we must disobey ourselves; and it is in this disobeying ourselves, wherein the hardness of obeying God consists."

# CRITICAL ESSAYS

# Major Themes

In a work of literature, a theme is a recurring, unifying subject or idea, a motif that helps us understand a work of art better. With a novel as richly ambiguous as *Moby-Dick*, we look at themes as guides, but it is important to be flexible while we do so. A good deal is left to individual interpretation so that one reader might disagree with another without necessarily being "wrong" or "right" about what the novel is saying. With that in mind, consider the following sections.

## Defiance

Because of the dominance of Ahab's quest in the novel, the theme of defiance is of paramount importance. Father Mapple prepares us for a consideration of defiance with his sermon about Jonah in Chapter 9. Jonah suffers from the sin of disobedience. When God asks him to submit to God's will, Jonah attempts to flee from god. He thinks that he can find some country where God does not rule. What he learns is that he must set aside his own wishes, his own vanity, if he is to follow God's way. Father Mapple puts it like this: "And if we obey god, we must disobey ourselves; and it is in this disobeying ourselves, wherein the hardness of obeying God consists."

Whether he is fighting against God or the rules of nature or some sort of perverse evil authority, Ahab is a defiant man. After Starbuck suggests that it is "blasphemous" to seek revenge on some poor dumb brute, such as a whale, when it merely followed instinct and took off the captain's leg, Ahab responds that he would "strike the sun if it insulted me" (Chapter 36). Ahab explains that he is not seeking revenge against a mere whale. He sees the White Whale as a mask, a façade, for his real enemy, which is an authority that rules over Ahab and which Ahab refuses to accept. The nature of that authority is debatable. We might infer that it is the order of nature, which Ahab sees as evil because Ahab insists on being placed higher in nature than a mere man can be.

Certainly Ahab is mad; even he knows that his monomaniacal obsession is not "normal." But he strikes us as not being a man who would *want* to be normal. Ahab strikes back against the inscrutable figure behind the mask because Ahab sees no justification for submitting to it. He rebels with anger because he wants to be more than he is. Ahab defies whatever authority there is and stands against it with a soul that can be killed but not defeated. In that sense, he condemns himself to death; but it is a death that he prefers to submission. In his madness and egocentrism, tragically, he takes his ship and most of his crew with him.

## Friendship

In contrast to Ahab's self-centered defiance is the theme of friendship, or camaraderie, which is characterized primarily through Ishmael and Queequeg. The two meet under awkward circumstances. As a result of a shortage of beds at the Spouter-Inn, as well as the mischievous nature of the proprietor, Queequeg and Ishmael find themselves in a frightening situation. Ishmael has no idea that his bunkmate is a "heathen" and concludes that the aborigine who enters the room late is a cannibal. Queequeg doesn't even know he is to share his bed with anyone and does threaten Ishmael's life. It's not an auspicious beginning for a friendship, but things soon get better because both men are open to the positive possibilities of diversity. They are characters who can and do grow and change. Queequeg left his native island of Kokovoko to learn about the rest of the world. Ishmael has similar motives for his ventures. Both understand that people from different cultures can learn from each other, and both value their differences as well as their similarities. An example is their respect for each other's religion. Although Queequeg is no Christian, he does attend services at the Whaleman's Chapel in New Bedford. Later, Ishmael bonds with Queequeg by sharing a pipe of tobacco and later making a burnt offering to Queequeg's little idol, Yojo.

Although it is not investigated in detail, this kind of friendship is also somewhat true of the crew of the *Pequod*, which is a microcosm of life from various cultures. Ishmael alludes to the camaraderie as he describes working whale blubber with the other men. Unfortunately, there are exceptions aboard ship. Stubb is one. His scene with the black cook, Fleece, may have been designed for humor; but it seems more like an illustration of the absence of brotherhood. The gams with other ships do provide positive opportunities for camaraderie. Significantly, Ahab has almost no interest in friendship. He eventually banishes the one person, Pip, who begins to get close to him. Ahab's mission allows for none of the warmth of friendship.

Ultimately, and symbolically, Queequeg indirectly saves Ishmael's life. It is Queequeg's coffin that pops to the surface after the *Pequod* sinks, providing the narrator with a life buoy and allowing him to survive until the *Rachel* rescues him. Queequeg could not have planned this, of course, but his loving nature would approve of his part in his friend's good fortune.

## Duty

Because most of the action of the novel takes place aboard ship, it is not surprising that duty is a major theme in *Moby-Dick*. The problem is how it is to be interpreted. For Father Mapple, the first duty of any shipmate is to God. We can serve our professional obligations only within that larger value system. This is not the case with Ahab. After Ahab's initial disagreement with Starbuck on the quarter-deck (Chapter 36) regarding the ship's mission, the crew sees Ahab as its highest authority. Later in the voyage, Ahab and Starbuck have another confrontation, again concerning duty, in the captain's cabin (Chapter 109).

Starbuck is a sincere Quaker with a hierarchy of loyalties: He feels a duty first to God, then to his employer (who supports Starbuck's family), then to his captain. When Starbuck discovers that some of the barrels in the hold of the ship must be leaking oil, he reports the situation to Ahab. The first mate expects the captain to stop the ship and turn all hands to a check of the casks because the ship's official mission is to capture whale oil and bring it home safely. As he says, "What we come twenty thousand miles to get is worth saving, sir." Ahab sardonically responds, "So it is, so it is; if we get it." Starbuck means the oil; Ahab means the White Whale. Starbuck reminds Ahab of the owners' interests, but the captain could not care less about the owners. He points a loaded musket toward the first mate and declares that there is "one Captain that is lord over the *Pequod*." Starbuck returns to the deck, and Ahab soon decides it is more prudent to stop the ship and make repairs.

It is clear, however, that the captain feels only one duty on this mission, and that is not to the owners or even to God but to Ahab. He will pursue his own monomaniacal goal in defiance of whatever gets in his path. The only way to stop Ahab is to kill him. When Starbuck has an opportunity to shoot the old man, with the same musket that Ahab pointed at him, the duties become confused in the first mate's mind. He has a duty to his family. How is that duty best served? He has a duty to the men who may well die with Ahab. But Starbuck feels a higher duty—to himself, to God, perhaps simply to decency. He is unable to pull the trigger, not through weakness but due to his own system of values. Because Starbuck cannot kill his captain, he must serve him.

## Death

Although it does not dominate until the end, the theme of death casts an ominous shadow over the novel. When Ishmael arrives at the Spouter-Inn, he immediately notices a large, obscure oil painting, a "boggy, soggy, squitchy picture" (Chapter 3) with such a confusion of shades and shadows that, for some time, he can make no sense of it. Contributing to the theme of death, and foreshadowing events later in the novel, the subject seems to be a ship foundering in a terrible storm and under attack from a whale. The inn's proprietor is named "Coffin," contributing symmetry to a book that begins and ends with a coffin.

From the first, Ahab appears to be familiar with death. He looks like a man "cut away from the stake, when the fire has overrunningly wasted all the limbs without consuming them" (Chapter 28). His mission has only two possible results: death for many of the men or victory over forces that probably cannot be defeated by this mortal. As practical as he is, Starbuck sees this; yet Starbuck cannot intentionally bring on his captain's death.

The *Pequod*'s voyage is a voyage to death, and the prophecies in the novel all anticipate it. Elijah, a prophet of doom, cryptically warns of dark endings before the ship sails. The Shaker prophet aboard the *Jeroboam*, who calls himself Gabriel, predicts that Ahab will soon be joining the dead at the bottom of the sea. Fedallah's prophecy is most elaborate as he details events leading up to and including Ahab's death. The Parsee's predictions all come true in unexpected ways.

The novel ends in death for all but the narrator, Ishmael, who lives to tell the tale because his friend Queequeg's coffin has been caulked and pitched to become a life buoy, which emerges from the vortex of the sunken *Pequod* to bring new life and hope to the narrator. In the first British publication, there was no epilogue explaining Ishmael's survival; a criticism of the story was that it was told by a dead man. Melville solved that problem with a poetic conclusion so ideal that it is difficult to imagine the novel without it.

While the themes add cohesion to the novel, it is important not to become lost in them. Above all, Ishmael has told us an excellent "yarn," as Father Mapple would say, and we should enjoy.

# Major Symbols

Symbols in literature are usually objects used to represent or suggest important concepts that inform and expand our appreciation of the work. *Moby-Dick* offers some of the most widely known symbols in American literature. Being widely known, however, does not imply that the symbols are simple or easy to understand. Like the themes in the novel, the symbols are ambiguous in enriching ways.

## Father Mapple's Pulpit

Father Mapple's pulpit in the Whaleman's Chapel effectively represents this former harpooner's approach to his ministry. Everything about the chapel reminds a visitor of life and death at sea. Father Mapple is the captain of the ship, the congregation his crew. The pulpit itself is shaped like the prow of a ship and features a painting of a vessel battling a storm near a rocky coast, an angel of hope watching over it. Without much effort, we can see that the pulpit represents the leadership of the pastor and implies that God himself is the pilot of this ship. Mapple's "shipmates," as he refers to the congregation, often find themselves battling storms on rocky coasts—either literally, in ships, or figuratively in the rest of their lives. They need the hope and consolation of God's grace, as represented by the angel.

Mapple ascends to the pulpit by climbing a rope ladder like one used to mount a ship from a boat at sea. He then pulls the rope up after him, effectively cutting off contact with worldly matters. In similar ways, the captain of a whaling ship assumes the pilot's role as he cuts off contact with land; the ship becomes a floating microcosm at sea. Melville makes effective use of contrast throughout the novel; here, it is between Mapple and Ahab. Mapple is an elderly but vigorous man of God who sees his role as leading his ship through rocky waters by gladly submitting to the will of a higher authority. Ahab is an ungodly man who doesn't mind wielding authority but resents submitting to it. He wears his defiance proudly. In this sense, the pulpit represents the proper position for a ship's captain, performing his duty in leading his congregation toward an understanding of performing God's will.

## Queequeg's coffin

The symbolism of Queequeg's coffin changes as the novel progresses. Initially, the coffin represents Queequeg's apparently impending death and his nostalgic link to his home island. The coffin is shaped like a canoe because of the custom on Kokovoko of setting the corpse adrift in such a craft. The belief was that eventually it would float over the ocean to the sky, which connects to the sea, and ultimately to one of the islands (stars) in the sky. Queequeg saw similar canoe coffins in Nantucket, and the custom of setting the corpse adrift is widespread among sea-faring people around the world.

The coffin represents ongoing life when it becomes Queequeg's sea chest after he decides not to die. It represents hope for renewal and a practical means of saving life when it is rigged to serve as a life buoy. Finally, the coffin is a symbol of hope and even rebirth when it springs from the vortex of the sunken *Pequod* to provide Ishmael with a means of staying afloat until the *Rachel* rescues him.

## The White Whale

The White Whale is one of the best known symbols in American literature. What it represents depends entirely on who is noticing. To Starbuck, Moby Dick is just another whale, except that he is more dangerous. Early in the novel, Starbuck challenges Ahab's motives for altering the ship's mission, from accumulating oil to killing the White Whale. On the quarter-deck in Chapter 36, Starbuck calls it "blasphemous" to seek revenge on a "dumb brute . . . that simply smote thee from blindest instinct!" If Starbuck sees anything beyond that in the whale, it is that Moby Dick represents the captain's madness and a very serious diversion from the ship's proper mission.

The *Samuel Enderby*'s captain, who has lost an arm to the White Whale, sees it as representing a great prize in both glory and sperm oil but seems very reasonable in his desire to leave the whale alone. He says to Ahab, "There would be great glory in killing him, I know that; and there is a ship-load of precious sperm in him, but, hark ye, he's best let alone; don't you think so, Captain?" (Chapter 100) Ahab points out that the "accursed thing is not always what least allures."

To some, the White Whale is a myth. To others, he is immortal. But one significant question is, What is the White Whale to Ahab? Ishmael grants that Ahab views the whale as an embodiment of evil. Ishmael himself is not so sure. The narrator often sees both sides of a question, never more so than in Chapter 42, "The Whiteness of the Whale." There he tells us that Moby Dick's whiteness might represent good or evil, glory or damnation, all colors or the "visible absence of color."

For Ahab's interpretation, it is helpful to consider the captain's comments in the pivotal Chapter 36. There, the captain says he sees Moby Dick as a "mask," behind which lies a great power whose dominance Ahab refuses to accept. Ahab sees that inscrutable power as evil. Some scholars argue that it is not the whale, or the force behind the whale, that is evil; the evil is in Ahab. Others see the captain as simply insane. Ahab is out of control as he rants about attacking the force behind the façade of Moby Dick. He wants to kill the whale in order to reach that force. Ahab seems to want to be a god. As great and charismatic a man as he can be in his finest moments, the captain is destructively egocentric and mad for power. To Ahab, we might conclude, the White Whale represents that power which limits and controls man. Ahab sees it as evil incarnate. But perhaps it is just a big, smart fish.

# CliffsNotes Review

Use this CliffsNotes Review to test your understanding of the original text and reinforce what you've learned in this book. After you work through the review and essay questions, identify the quote section, and the fun and useful practice projects, you're well on your way to understanding a comprehensive and meaningful interpretation of *Moby-Dick*.

## Q&A

**1.** The *Pequod* is named after

    **a.** a type of whale

    **b.** a New England seaport

    **c.** an extinct Massachusetts Indian tribe

**2.** Queequeg's native island is called

    **a.** Oahu

    **b.** Kokovoko

    **c.** Maui

**3.** The second mate on the *Pequod* is

    **a.** Wilson

    **b.** Starbuck

    **c.** Stubb

**4.** The harpooner whom Queequeg rescues is named

    **a.** Fedallah

    **b.** Tashtego

    **c.** Starbuck

**5.** The ship that rescues Ishmael at the end of the novel is the

    **a.** *Rachel*

    **b.** *Minnow*

    **c.** *Bachelor*

**6.** Ahab's personal harpooner and spiritual guide is named _____.

**7.** _____ delivers his sermon at the Whaleman's Chapel.

**8.** Of all types of whale, Ishmael values the _____ whale most highly.

**9.** The "doubloon" is offered to the first man to _____.

**10.** Queequeg's casket is originally in the shape of a _____.

**Answers:** (1) c. (2) b. (3) c. (4) b. (5) a. (6) Fedallah (7) Father Mapple (8) sperm (9) spot ("raise") Moby Dick (10) canoe

# Identify the Quote

**1.** Who-e debel you? . . . you no speak-e, dam-me, I kill-e.

**2.** Vengeance on a dumb brute! . . . that simply smote thee from blindest instinct! Madness! To be enraged with a dumb thing . . . seems blasphemous.

**3.** If man will strike, strike through the mask! . . . That inscrutable thing is chiefly what I hate.

**4.** And if we obey God, we must disobey ourselves; and it is in this disobeying ourselves, wherein the hardness of obeying God consists.

**5.** What is it, what nameless, inscrutable, unearthly thing is it; what cozening, hidden lord and master, and cruel, remorseless emperor commands me? . . . Is Ahab, Ahab?

**6.** Buoyed up by that coffin, for almost one whole day and night, I floated on a soft and dirge-like main . . . . On the second day, a sail drew near, nearer, and picked me up at last. It was the devious-cruising *Rachel*, that in her retracing search after her missing children, only found another orphan.

**7.** Hast seen the White Whale?

**8.** Call me Ishmael.

**9.** Though it come to the last, I shall still go before thee thy pilot . . . . Hemp only can kill thee.

**10.** What is best let alone, that accursed thing is not always what least allures. He's all a magnet!

**Answers:** (1) [Queequeg discovers Ishmael in his bed at the Spouter-Inn.] (2) [Starbuck confronts Ahab regarding the mission of the *Pequod* in Chapter 36.] (3) [Ahab responds to Starbuck, discussing the nature of the thing he seeks to kill.] (4) [Father Mapple articulates the theme of his sermon.] (5) [Ahab considers what drives him.] (6) [Ishmael addresses the reader for the last time, explaining his rescue.] (7) [Ahab's usual greeting, and only interest, in meeting another ship.] (8) [The narrator's opening line to the novel is one of the best known in American literature.] (9) [This is Fedallah's prophecy to Ahab.] (10) [Ahab responds to the captain of the Samuel Enderby, regarding Moby Dick.]

# Essay Questions

1. Discuss the role of diversity as it affects the theme of friendship in the novel.

2. Consider the characters of Ishmael, Starbuck, and Ahab. Which are static characters, and which ones grow or change throughout the novel? How is this growth (or lack of growth) shown?

3. What does Pip see when he is left alone at sea? How does it change him?

4. The *Pequod* has several gams at sea. Define a "gam" and discuss the importance of any one gam that occurs during the course of the novel.

5. Why does Ahab want to kill the White Whale?

6. Describe Ahab's physical appearance and discuss how this adds to the impression of the character.

7. Stubb is usually thought of as a carefree, fun-loving guy. Describe what you think of him and use scenes from the novel to ilustrate your impression.

8. What is Fedallah's role in the novel?

9. Discuss the following as symbols: the White Whale, Queequeg's coffin, and Father Mapple's pulpit.

10. How does Father Mapple's sermon set the tone for the novel?

# Practice Projects

**1.** Pretend that you are Ishmael. Write a two-page report of an event at your school, or in the community, emulating as closely as possible his narrative style.

**2.** If you could interview any of the characters halfway through the novel, which one would you choose? What would you like to ask? What answers would you probably receive?

**3.** If you could change any single aspect of the style or the plot of *Moby-Dick*, what would it be? How would you change it?

**4.** As a class project, divide into small groups with each presenting a scene from the novel as a short play.

**5.** Design your own Web site about *Moby-Dick* and describe what contents you would feature.

# CliffsNotes Resource Center

The learning doesn't need to stop here. CliffsNotes Resource Center shows you the best of the best—links to the best information in print and online about the author and/or related works. And don't think that this is all we've prepared for you; we've put all kinds of pertinent information at www.cliffsnotes.com. Look for all the terrific resources at your favorite bookstore or local library and on the Internet. When you're online, make your first stop www.cliffsnotes.com where you'll find more incredibly useful information about *Moby-Dick*.

## Books

This CliffsNotes book provides a meaningful interpretation of *Moby-Dick*. If you are looking for information about the author and/or related works, check out these other publications:

*Ahab,* edited by Harold Bloom. One of the Major Critical Characters series, this volume presents insightful extracts and essays that are very helpful to the student seeking a deeper understanding of Ahab. The editor's personal introduction is of special interest. New York: Chelsea House Publishers, 1991.

*Herman Melville's Moby-Dick,* edited by Harold Bloom. A part of the Major Critical Interpretations series, this collection includes several of the most perceptive analyses of the novel, including Charles Olson's seminal metaphorical piece as well as Henry A. Murray's consideration of "*In Nomine Diaboli*." With an introduction by the editor. New York: Chelsea House Publishers, 1986.

*A Herman Melville Encyclopedia,* by Robert L. Gale. This extremely helpful resource volume contains entries on characters, works, and relatives and associates of the author. With a thorough chronology, the book is very reliable. Westport, Connecticut: Greenwood Press, 1995.

*Critical Essays on Herman Melville's Moby-Dick,* edited by Brian Higgins and Hershel Parker. If the student had to rely on just one secondary source for the novel, this would be a good choice. Featured are early reviews, essays by key literary figures (D. H. Lawrence,

Virginia Woolf), and a wide assortment of articles, critiques, and personal responses. A delightful, fun, informative book. Highly recommended. New York: G. K. Hall & Co., 1992.

*Moby-Dick: Ishmael's Mighty Book,* by Kerry McSweeney. This is a good place to start for any student assigned a research paper. The sections on historical background and composition are helpful, as is the annotated bibliography. Some early reviews are noted. Boston: Twayne Publishers, 1886.

*A Reading of Moby-Dick,* by M. O. Percival. A charmingly perceptive study by one of the best Melville scholars, this small (129 pages) volume holds up very well over time and is as worthwhile an introduction as a beginning student could find. Chicago: University of Chicago Press, 1950.

It's easy to find books published by IDG Books Worldwide, Inc. You'll find them in your favorite bookstores (on the Internet and at a store near you). We also have three Web sites that you can use to read about all the books we publish:

- www.cliffsnotes.com

- www.dummies.com

- www.idgbooks.com

# Internet

Check out these Web resources for more information about Herman Melville and *Moby-Dick*:

**The Life and Works of Herman Melville,** http://www.melville. org/—This is an extensive and very interesting site featuring information on current Melville events, biography, electronic texts, and criticism, as well as references to other related sites on the Web. Highly recommended.

**Western Canon University,** http://mobydicks.com or http:// westerncanon.com—Through the Western Canon University site, the student can access the "Herman Melville Discussion Deck" as well as a variety of offerings on Melville's works and characters.

**Whales in Literature,** www.keele.ac.uk/depts/as/Literature/ Moby-Dick/amlit.whale-pages.html—This site offers links to the complete text of *Moby-Dick,* as well as links to whale watching and conservation groups. The site also includes original introductory material (a dedication to Nathaniel Hawthorne, an entymology of the word "whale," and extracts from world literature regarding whales) that Melville included but many publishers do not.

**Herman Melville & Moby Dick Campfire Chat,** `killdevilhill.com/melvillechat/wwwboard.html`—This site offers a message board "devoted to the life and works of Herman Melville, ranging from Moby Dick to Billy Budd to Pierre."

Next time you're on the Internet, don't forget to drop by `www.cliffsnotes.com`. We created an online Resource Center that you can use today, tomorrow, and beyond.

# Periodicals

Following are some articles that you may find interesting or enlightening as you study *Moby-Dick:*

AUDEN, W. H. "The Christian Tragic Hero." *New York Times Book Review,* 16 December 1945: 1, 21. A controversial reading of the novel as a Christian tragedy, this article presents a unique view of Ahab by one of the great poets of recent centuries.

BROOKS, VAN WYCK. "A Reviewer's Notebook." *Freeman* 7, 16 May 1923: 238–39. One of the important critical assessments of the novel in the 1920s, this by a highly respected critic; the short article helps to encourage extensive scholarship.

PATTERSON, MARK R. "Democratic Leadership and Narrative Authority in *Moby-Dick.*" *Studies in The Novel* 16 (1984): 288–303. Ishmael is considered in light of the expansion of democracy in mid-nineteenth century America.

# Films

*Moby-Dick.* A Whale/Nine Network Australia Production, 1998. Directed by Franc Roddam and starring Patrick Stewart as Ahab and Henry Thomas as Ishmael. Although some specifics cannot be relied upon, the film does accurately present the tone and many of the facts of the novel. Gregory Peck's Father Mapple is not to be missed.

*Moby-Dick.* A Warner Brothers-Moulin Production, 1956. Directed by John Huston and starring Gregory Peck as Ahab and Richard Basehart as Ishmael. The special effects are dated, and some facts are misrepresented. For its time, this is an impressive work by a legendary director. Orson Welles plays Father Mapple.

## Audio Recordings

*Moby-Dick.* Harper Audio, 1998. Abridged (93 minutes), featuring Charlton Heston. A popular version, this may be available through bookstores or libraries.

*Moby-Dick.* Dove Audio, 1996. Abridged (360 minutes), featuring Burt Reynolds. Another popular version, usually somewhat more expensive than the Harper Audio.

*Moby-Dick.* Durkin Hayes Publishing, Ltd., 1986. Abridged (180 minutes), featuring George Kennedy.

*Moby-Dick.* Books on Tape, 1984. Unabridged, featuring Walter Zimmerman. This complete, more expensive version may be available through libraries.

## Send Us Your Favorite Tips

In your quest for knowledge, have you ever experienced that sublime moment when you figure out a trick that saves time or trouble? Perhaps you realized you were taking ten steps to accomplish something that could have taken two. Or you found a little-known workaround that achieved great results. If you've discovered a useful resource that gave you insight into or helped you understand *Moby-Dick* and you'd like to share it, the CliffsNotes staff would love to hear from you. Go to our Web site at www.cliffsnotes.com and click the Talk to Us button. If we select your tip, we may publish it as part of CliffsNotes Daily, our exciting, free e-mail newsletter. To find out more or to subscribe to a newsletter, go to on the Web.

# INDEX

## A

## B

## C

# NOTES